The Best of Casual Italian Cooking

TRATTORIA

SUNSET BOOKS
President and Publisher: Susan J. Maruyama
Director, Finance and Business Affairs: Gary Loebner
Director, Manufacturing and Sales Service: Lorinda Reichert
Director, Sales and Marketing: Richard A. Smeby
Editorial Director: Kenneth Winchester
Executive Editor: Robert A. Doyle

SUNSET PUBLISHING CORPORATION
Chairman: Jim Nelson
President/Chief Executive Officer: Robin Wolaner
Chief Financial Officer: James E. Mitchell
Publisher: Stephen J. Seabolt
Circulation Director: Robert I. Gursha
Editor, *Sunset Magazine:* William R. Marken

Produced by
WELDON OWEN INC.
President: John Owen
Publisher and Vice President: Wendely Harvey
Managing Editor: Lisa Chaney Atwood
Consulting Editor: Norman Kolpas
Copy Editor: Sharon Silva
Design: Patty Hill
Production Director: Stephanie Sherman
Production Editor: Janique Gascoigne
Co-Editions Director: Derek Barton
Co-Editions Production Manager (US): Tarji Mickelson
Food Photography: Peter Johnson
Assistant Food Photographer: Dal Harper
Food Stylist: Janice Baker
Assistant Food Stylists: Amanda Biffin, Liz Nolan, Alison Turner
Cover Photography: Joyce Oudkerk Pool
Cover Food Stylist: Susan Massey
Cover Prop Stylist: Carol Hacker
Half-Title Illustration: Martha Anne Booth
Chapter Opener Illustrations: Dorothy Reinhardt
Glossary Illustrations: Alice Harth

Production by Kyodo Printing Co.
(S'pore) Pte Ltd
Printed in Singapore

ISBN 0-376-02038-5
Library of Congress Catalog Card Number: 95-067091

A Note on Weights and Measures:
All recipes include customary U.S. and metric measurements.
Metric conversions are based on a standard developed for these
books and have been rounded off. Actual weights may vary.

The Best of Casual Italian Cooking

TRATTORIA

by Mary Beth Clark

Contents

Introduction 7

Appetizers 17

First Courses 33

Main Courses 65

Side Dishes 89

Desserts 101

Introduction

Walking along cobbled streets, you're suddenly surrounded with enticing aromas emanating from a warm and inviting neighborhood restaurant. Seated inside at one table are a group of friends laughing and relaxing together; at another, three generations of a local family are engaged in spirited conversation, while eating their meal with obvious pleasure.

This is an Italian trattoria, a place where all can enjoy home cooking away from home in an atmosphere that can be as casual and natural as a gathering around the kitchen table. The menu commonly features a variety of regional specialties made from seasonal ingredients grown by local farmers. The cook and wait staff are usually family members who often know both the names and the preferences of their customers.

All these elements combine to make the trattoria the ideal establishment for a quick lunch alone during the workweek, a simple dinner with a gathering of friends, or a birthday or anniversary celebration with the entire family. Simply put, the trattoria is Italy's customary place to *mangia bene*—eat well—in comfortable and welcoming surroundings.

Trattoria History

Trattorias began as family businesses, extensions of the home kitchen. For centuries, Italy was basically an agrarian economy and Italian laborers were often forced to move in search of work. Unification of the country was not achieved until the 1860s, so the people who settled in new towns were often regarded as immigrants. Because work was generally difficult to find, some of these newcomers sought to stabilize their livelihood by turning to what they knew best, home cooking. A family would crowd into the upstairs of the house and convert the ground floor into a restaurant. Using recipes that had been handed down by word-of-mouth, grandmothers and mothers served home-style meals in these renovated spaces, with every dish made from scratch. The older children waited on the tables, while the men tended crops or worked other jobs.

Serving fresh, delicious, affordable food, these neighborhood restaurants quickly became the place for locals to go for lunch or dinner when not eating at home. Today, many trattorias continue to serve *cucina casalinga*—home-style cooking—as well as the fresh, lighter fare now popular in Italy. These establishments often remain family businesses today, with different family members pitching in to perform more than one job. Sometimes two restaurant families unite through marriage, making for an even larger trattoria with a longer menu.

Trattorias offer visitors a way of connecting with the lives of the residents, and the restaurants themselves are a true reflection of the local culture. Wherever you travel in Italy, the cooking changes with the dialect, and it is in the trattorias that you will find the most authentic local dishes.

The Trattoria Experience

Each of Italy's twenty regions has its own culinary style. As in years past, climate and geography still determine seasonal specialties. In general, trattoria cooks in the rich agricultural north with its cooler weather use more butter, goat's milk cheeses, polenta, rice, fresh pasta, meat and game. In the warmer south, including the islands of Sicily and Sardinia,

TRATTORIA: THE BEST OF CASUAL ITALIAN COOKING

olive oil, dried pasta, seafood dishes and sheep's milk cheeses are common features on restaurant menus.

The trattoria's *menu del giorno*, or "daily menu," is a list of the chef's specialties based primarily on what the market offers that day. The food shopping is accomplished in the early morning hours at outdoor markets, where vendors display an assortment of locally harvested vegetables and ripe fruits. Depending on the season, wild greens, mushrooms and game, as well as fresh seafood, may also be sold in the market stalls.

In addition to its daily specialties, the trattoria table is often graced with a basket of the dense and crusty local bread, thin and crisp breadsticks known as *grissini* or tender pieces of the flat bread known as *focaccia.* A bottle of extra-virgin olive oil is often

set alongside, for drizzling over sliced bread, as well as grilled vegetables, meats and seafood.

A typical trattoria meal is served in courses, with the wines often changing to suit each new plate. The feast begins with an appetizer and drink—*antipasto* and *aperitivo*—to whet the appetite. The next course, the *primo piatto,* is a grain dish of pasta, risotto or polenta or, in some cases, a *minestra,* or "soup." Then comes the *secondo piatto,* the main course of poultry, meat or fish, often simply prepared. Seasonal vegetables serve as the side dishes, or *contorni,* and are ordered separately. Desserts, or *dolci,* range from wedges of cheese or pieces of ripe fruit to luscious pastries, sometimes accompanied by a dessert wine. A steaming hot espresso and perhaps a liqueur, *digestivo* or *grappa* cap the meal.

Inside the trattorias in Italy today, the decor ranges from simple to refined. The more informal operations have a rustic country style, limited menus and often occupy the lower floors of houses. Such restaurants derive some of their charm from their exposed wooden beams and spare shelves holding family memorabilia, religious statuary and copper pots. Hand-painted earthenware plates adorn the walls and often double as serving pieces. Plain wooden or marble tables are topped with paper placemats or red-and-white-checkered tablecloths, glass tumblers and a carafe of house wine. Menus are

recited by the waiter or written on a blackboard and feature just a few local dishes served on thick, white ceramic plates.

The more gentrified trattorias provide intimate dining at pastel linen–covered tables set with crystal wine goblets. An *aperitivo* can usually be sipped at a small bar before you are seated. Side tables are laden with seasonal produce, *antipasti* and *dolci*

prepared that day. Sometimes there is outdoor seating, with tables nestled under the protection of a grape arbor or topped with colorful umbrellas. A neatly printed menu offers both traditional and lighter fare in addition to a selection of fine regional wines.

No matter whether you choose hand-painted earthenware on a checkered tablecloth or porcelain on fine linen, the recipes that follow will give your home-cooked trattoria meal an authentic Italian flavor.

Beverages

Traditionally, the most festive way to begin a meal is with an *aperitivo,* most commonly a flute of dry sparkling white wine such as Prosecco, Spumante or Asti Spumante Brut. If you like, flavor it with white-peach purée to make a Bellini (see opposite page), or add drops of thick, mahogany-colored, well-aged balsamic vinegar. Increasingly popular are nonalcoholic drinks made from fresh fruits or syrups, such as strawberry purée or almond syrup mixed with sparkling water. Also chic are nonalcoholic bitters, such as Crodino, flavored with a green olive. Many people love mixed drinks that combine bitters, Campari and soda. You might also try a Negroni (Campari, sweet red vermouth and gin garnished with an orange or lemon slice) or an Americano (Campari, sweet red vermouth and soda) or pungent artichoke-based Cynar served over ice. Offer small bowls of roasted almonds, chunks of Parmesan, green olives, cubes of mortadella, or other *antipasti* along with the *aperitivi.*

Wines

Italy produces more than one-fifth of the world's wine. Aside from the hundreds of professional winemakers, most Italians who grow grapes make their own wines for family consumption, either at home or at the town cooperative. Many of Italy's most famous wines originated in just this manner, with the grandfather doing the first planting and crushing.

Refined through the generations, these fine wines are now classified under Italian law as *denominazione di origine controllata* (DOC) and *denominazione di origine controllata e garantita* (DOCG), with the latter designating the highest rank. The remainder are classified as *vino da tavola,* although many of these are superior wines as well.

Among the best dry white wine varieties are Gavi, Pinot Grigio, Pinot Bianco and Orvieto, which are all especially good with *antipasti,* light pastas and risottos. Slightly fruity whites, such as Soave, Müller-Thurgau and Tocai, complement dishes that feature herbs, as well as soups, pastas, vegetables, poultry and fish. Slightly *frizzante* (sparkling) whites, particularly Verdicchio and Pinot Bianco, are wonderful with fish and shellfish, while such reds as Lambrusco Grasparossa or Lambrusco di Sorbara marry well with meat dishes and cream sauces.

Lighter, fruitier reds, including Sangiovese, Dolcetto d'Alba, Barbera d'Asti and Valpolicella, are excellent with pastas, pizzas, fish, chicken and veal. The full-bodied red wines of

Tuscany—Chianti Classico Riserva, Brunello di Montalcino—and Piedmont's robust Barolo and Barbaresco complement pasta with ragù, meats and game dishes. A variety of new-style wines, such as the Tuscan Cabernet-blended reds Sassicaia, Ornellaia and Solaia, are delicious with meat and game as well.

Every November, Italians eagerly await the arrival on trattoria tables of two bottles from recent harvests. One is filled with just-pressed, peppery and herbaceous extra-virgin olive oil. The other holds *vino novello,* red wine bottled no more than a year, and often only a few months after crushing. Both have a bold freshness that pairs well with trattoria cooking.

A sparkling wine, such as sweet Asti Spumante, Moscato d'Asti or Brachetto d'Acqui, frequently accompanies dessert.

A wholly different pleasure are the still dessert wines made from *passito,* or semi-dried grapes. Whereas the sparkling wines match up well with selections from the dessert tray, the richer and sweeter still dessert wines are usually sipped alone or with a plate of fresh fruit or crisp *biscotti.* Among the best are Moscato di Pantelleria, Verduzzo di Ramandolo, Malvasia delle Lipari and Vin Santo.

After-Dinner Drinks

The Italians take their espresso very seriously. They use only superior-quality coffee beans, roast them to an exacting formula and brew them with plain mineral water in a specially designed machine. The revered liquid is then served in thick porcelain cups following—never with—dessert. *Caffè corretto,* an espresso with a dash of liqueur or *grappa,* is a popular variation.

Each region and even some cities make their own *digestivo,* a mildly bitter herbal liqueur that Italians believe aids the digestion if drunk at the meal's end. Fernet Branca, Sicilian Averna and Millefiori are among those to try. Or you may wish to sample some of Italy's famed *grappa,* a strong liquor distilled from the grape pomace. Sweet liqueurs, such as almond-flavored amaretto and anise-flavored sambuca, and fortified wines, including aged sweet Marsala, are also popular.

BELLINI

Created by Giuseppe Cipriani of Harry's Bar in Venice, this is probably one of Italy's most popular aperitivi. A few drops of raspberry purée impart rich color and flavor to the drink. If white peaches are not available, use yellow peach purée and omit the raspberry.

⅔ cup (5 fl oz/160 ml) white-peach purée

1 teaspoon raspberry purée

1 bottle (24 fl oz/750 ml) chilled Prosecco, Asti Spumante Brut or other Italian sparkling dry white wine

♣ In the bottom of each flute or white-wine glass, pour about 1½ tablespoons peach purée and add 2 or 3 drops of raspberry purée. Pour an equal amount of the wine into each glass and serve immediately.

Serves 6

Basic Recipes

Just a handful of essential recipes provide a foundation for casual Italian cooking. Few trattoria meals would be complete without a light egg or spinach pasta and a robust tomato sauce. And to enhance the flavor of soups, stews, sauces and braises, a good homemade stock should always be close at hand.

MAKING FRESH PASTA

The classic pasta dough, or sfoglia, of Emilia-Romagna requires only two ingredients, flour and eggs. Bleached all-purpose flour yields a more tender dough than the unbleached variety. The dough can be made by hand or in a food processor, then rolled out with a wooden rolling pin or by machine. You can make pasta dough up to 2 days ahead. Or, if short of time, purchase ready-made fresh pasta sheets and cut as directed in individual recipes.

BASIC EGG PASTA
2   cups (10 oz/315 g) all-purpose (plain) flour, or as needed
4   large eggs, plus beaten egg as needed

SPINACH PASTA *(see opposite page)*
1¾ lb (875 g) spinach, stems removed (14 oz/440 g trimmed)
3   cups (15 oz/470 g) all-purpose (plain) flour, or as needed
2   large eggs, plus beaten egg as needed

Mixing the Dough

▣ *To mix the basic egg pasta by hand,* on a clean work surface, place the 2 cups (10 oz/315 g) flour in a mound. Make a well in the center and add the 4 eggs to the well. Using a fork, beat the eggs, gradually incorporating small amounts of the flour from the interior wall of the well into the eggs. Working in a circular pattern, continue to incorporate flour, being careful to maintain the wall of flour so the eggs do not run over the edge.

▣ Work the flour into the eggs until a smooth dough forms. Depending on the humidity, a little less or a little more flour may be needed. If less flour is needed, simply don't incorporate all of it; if more is needed, sprinkle a little on top of the dough and knead it in.

▣ On a clean surface, knead the dough until smooth, velvety and elastic, 1–2 minutes. Cover with a bowl to prevent drying and let the dough relax for 1 hour before rolling it out.

▣ *To mix the basic egg pasta in a food processor,* place the 2 cups (10 oz/315 g) flour in a food processor fitted with the metal blade. In a bowl, lightly whisk the eggs just until blended. Turn on the food processor to aerate the flour briefly, then pour in the eggs. Continue to process for a few seconds until the dough can be pressed into a ball. If the dough is too dry, add beaten egg, 1 teaspoon at a time, and pulse until the correct consistency is achieved. If too moist, add flour, 2 tablespoons at a time, and pulse. Remove the dough from the processor and knead briefly until the surface is smooth, velvety and elastic, 1–2 minutes. Cover with a bowl to prevent drying and let the dough relax for 1 hour before rolling it out.

▣ Use the pasta dough immediately, or wrap airtight and refrigerate for up to 2 days. Before using, unwrap the dough, cover with a bowl to prevent drying and bring to room temperature.

Rolling and Cutting the Dough

▣ *To roll out and cut the dough with a pasta machine,* cut the dough in half or thirds. Cover unused dough with a bowl to prevent drying. Set the pasta machine rollers to their widest opening (number 1 on most machines) and feed one portion of the dough through the rollers. Roll through once, fold the dough crosswise into thirds, turn it a quarter turn and roll through again. Then roll the sheet through one more time to strengthen the dough. Set the rollers to the next smaller opening and roll the dough through once. Continue in this manner, progressively setting the rollers to the next smaller opening and rolling the dough through once. On the first, third and fifth settings (numbers 1, 3 and 5), roll through twice to strengthen the dough. Roll out the dough to a thickness of ⅛ or 1/16 inch (3 mm or 2 mm), the second-to-last and last settings on most machines, as specified in each recipe.

▣ If the dough ripples, too much dough is being pushed through the rollers or the dough isn't relaxed enough to be stretched. Cover the pasta sheet and allow it to relax for a few minutes, then return to the previous setting and roll through. If the dough repeatedly breaks, the gluten must be developed more. Knead the dough by hand and let it relax as before, then begin the rolling again.

For flat cuts such as pappardelle and tagliatelle, place the pasta sheet on a lightly floured board and let dry a little for easier cutting (15–20 minutes) while you roll out the remaining dough. Then adjust the blades to the desired width as directed in individual recipes and pass the sheets through the cutters. Gently separate the pasta strands and gather loosely into small piles. Let dry for 1 hour. Meanwhile, cut the remaining pasta sheets.

To roll out and cut the dough by hand, divide the dough in half or thirds. Cover unused dough with a bowl to prevent drying. On a lightly floured board, roll out one portion of the dough ⅛–⅟₁₆-inch (3–2-mm) thick, or as specified in each recipe.

For flat cuts such as pappardelle and tagliatelle, place the pasta sheet on a lightly floured board; let dry a little for easy cutting (15–20 minutes) while you roll out the remaining dough. Using 1 pasta sheet at a time and beginning at a long end, loosely roll up the dough, making folds every 2½ inches (6 cm). Cut the roll crosswise into slices the width of pasta specified in each recipe. Gently separate the pasta strands and gather loosely into small piles. Let dry for 1 hour. Meanwhile, cut the remaining pasta sheets.

For filled pasta, use the pasta sheets made by either the machine or hand method immediately to prevent drying, filling and cutting the pasta dough as directed in individual recipes.

Making Spinach Pasta

Rinse the spinach and place in a steamer rack over (not touching) boiling water. Cover and steam, stirring occasionally, until wilted and tender, 4–5 minutes. Transfer to a colander to drain, pressing against the spinach with the back of a spoon and then squeezing it with your hands to remove the excess water.

In a food processor fitted with the metal blade or in a blender, purée the spinach until smooth. Transfer to paper towels; squeeze to remove any remaining moisture. You should have about ¾ cup (5 oz/155 g) spinach.

Follow the directions for basic egg pasta, adding the spinach with the eggs if mixing the dough by hand and with the flour if mixing it in a food processor. Continue to roll and cut the dough as directed for basic egg pasta.

Makes about 17 oz (530 g) basic egg pasta and 1½ lb (750 g) spinach pasta

FISH STOCK

BRODO DI PESCE

Fish stock tastes best when made with a combination of fish and shellfish. Frozen fish stock, available in some well-stocked food stores, is the best substitute.

1   tablespoon unsalted butter
2   lb (1 kg) cod, halibut or haddock steaks
6   oz (185 g) shrimp (prawns) in the shell or scallops
1   celery stalk, cut in half
2   thick slices yellow onion
1   cup (8 fl oz/250 ml) fruity Italian white wine
5   cups (40 fl oz/1.25 l) cold water
1   bay leaf
½   teaspoon fresh thyme leaves or ¼ teaspoon dried thyme
8   fresh parsley stems

▣ In a deep saucepan over medium heat, melt the butter. Add the fish and shrimp or scallops and sauté until opaque, 2–3 minutes.

▣ Add the celery, onion and wine. Bring to a boil over high heat and boil for 1 minute. Add the water and return to a boil. Using a large spoon, skim any scum from the surface. Add the bay leaf, thyme and parsley stems. Reduce the heat to low and simmer, uncovered, for 18–20 minutes; do not overcook.

▣ Strain the stock through a fine-mesh sieve lined with cheesecloth (muslin) into a clean container. Use immediately, or let cool, cover and refrigerate for up to 12 hours or freeze for up to 2 weeks.

Makes about 5 cups (40 fl oz/1.25 l)

MEAT STOCK

BRODO DI CARNE

A variety of raw meats imparts a subtle depth of flavor and lightness to this versatile stock. The caramelized onion, cheese rind and tomato add to the satisfying richness. Purchased beef stock can replace homemade when you are pressed for time.

1   yellow onion
1   chicken, 3 lb (1.5 kg), cut into 8 pieces
1   lb (500 g) beef shank with bone
½   lb (250 g) veal stew meat, cut into large cubes
1   large carrot, peeled
1   celery stalk
4   qt (4 l) cold water
2   small pieces rind from Italian Parmesan cheese, about 1 oz (30 g) total weight
1   plum (Roma) tomato

▣ Skewer the whole onion on a fork and hold it over an open flame on the stove top until its skin turns a dark gold. Alternatively, preheat a broiler (griller) and broil (grill) the onion until the edges are lightly browned.

▣ In a deep stockpot, combine the chicken, beef, veal, browned onion, carrot and celery. Add the water and bring to a boil over high heat. Using a large spoon, skim any scum from the surface. Reduce the heat to low, cover partially and simmer for 2 hours.

▣ Add the cheese rind and tomato and simmer, uncovered, for 1 hour longer to blend the flavors; do not overcook and do not allow to boil.

▣ Remove from the heat and strain through a fine-mesh sieve lined with cheesecloth (muslin) into a clean container. Use immediately, or let cool, cover and refrigerate for up to 5 days or freeze for up to 1 month. Before using the chilled stock, lift off and discard the fat congealed on the surface.

Makes about 2¾ qt (2.75 l)

VEGETABLE STOCK
BRODO DI VERDURA

You can use this full-bodied vegetable stock in place of any meat or fish stock. Purchased vegetable stock can be used in place of homemade when time is short.

2   tablespoons extra-virgin olive oil
1   cup (5 oz/155 g) diced carrot
¾   cup (4 oz/125 g) diced celery
¾   cup (2 oz/60 g) sliced leeks
1   small clove garlic
1   small red (Spanish) onion, cut in half
¾   lb (375 g) fresh white mushrooms, cut in halves
8   cups (64 fl oz/2 l) cold water
1   small plum (Roma) tomato
½   teaspoon fresh thyme leaves or ¼ teaspoon dried thyme
½   teaspoon fresh marjoram leaves or ¼ teaspoon dried marjoram
4   fresh parsley sprigs
    Salt and freshly ground pepper

◫ In a saucepan over low heat, warm the olive oil. Add the carrot, celery and leeks and sauté until the leeks are slightly translucent, 3–4 minutes.

◫ Add the garlic, onion and mushrooms and sauté until the onion is slightly translucent, about 2 minutes.

◫ Pour in the water and bring to a boil over high heat. Using a large spoon, skim any scum from the surface, if necessary. Add the tomato, thyme, marjoram and parsley. Reduce the heat to low and simmer, uncovered, until the flavors are blended, about 1 hour.

◫ Strain the stock through a fine-mesh sieve lined with cheesecloth (muslin) into a clean container. Season to taste with salt and pepper. Use immediately, or let cool, cover and refrigerate for up to 3 days or freeze for up to 1 month.

Makes about 5 cups (40 fl oz/1.25 l)

QUICK TOMATO SAUCE
SALSA RAPIDA DI POMODORO

This fresh-tasting tomato sauce cooks in less than 1 hour. It will have its freshest flavor when served within a few hours of preparation, but it can be covered and refrigerated for 1–2 days or frozen for up to 2 weeks and still be delicious. If you like, add garlic and herbs and/or a few tablespoons of red or white wine to the sauce near the end of cooking.

2   tablespoons extra-virgin olive oil or sunflower or canola oil
¼   cup (1¼ oz/37 g) finely chopped yellow onion
    Minced garlic, optional
    Minced fresh or dried herbs, optional
6   cups (36 oz/1.1 kg) peeled, seeded, chopped and well-drained plum (Roma) tomatoes (fresh or canned)
    Salt and ground white pepper

◫ In a saucepan over low heat, warm the oil. Add the onion and sauté until translucent, 4–5 minutes; do not allow to brown. Add garlic and herbs to taste (or as directed in individual recipes) and sauté until fragrant, about 1 minute.

◫ Add the tomatoes and bring to a boil over high heat. Reduce the heat to low and simmer uncovered, stirring occasionally, until thickened and the juices have evaporated, 30–35 minutes for canned tomatoes and 40–45 minutes for fresh tomatoes.

◫ Season to taste with salt and white pepper. Use immediately, or let cool, cover and refrigerate or freeze.

Makes about 2 cups (16 fl oz/500 ml)

Appetizers

J ust inside the door of most trattorias stands a table arrayed with the day's offering of *antipasti*—a warm welcome to all who enter. These appetizers glisten with freshness and hold the promise of a delectable meal to come. They are intended to whet the appetite, take the edge off the most ravenous hunger and complement the rest of the repast. This course may be limited to a single dish, or it may comprise two or three different selections made from those on display.

There are two basic categories of *antipasti,* those served cold and those presented hot. Both groups often reflect the region and season in which they are offered. *Antipasti* are usually based on vegetables, cheese or shellfish, with meat generally only a light accent. The most important characteristics of any *antipasti,* however, are that the preparations be simple and the ingredients perfectly fresh.

Whether you opt for a slice of toasted bread topped with tomatoes, a crisp salad or a skewer of grilled fresh shrimp, the *antipasto* offers a hint of the savory flavors to come. Enjoyed with an *aperitivo,* it is all you need to stave off the pangs of hunger until the first course arrives.

Sicilian Smoked Fish and Orange Salad

Typically Sicilian in its mixture of savory and sweet flavors, this dish is at its best in winter, when oranges are slightly tart and contrast vividly with the smoked fish and creamy cheese. Smoked trout makes an excellent substitute for the whitefish.

2 whole smoked whitefish, such as smoked chub, 1¼ lb (625 g) total weight

2 large juice oranges, peeled and all white pith removed

12 oil-cured black olives, pitted and cut in halves

6 oz (185 g) caciotta, provolone or Gouda cheese, rind removed and cut into ½-inch (12-mm) cubes

2 green (spring) onions, thinly sliced

2 tablespoons fresh oregano leaves or 2 teaspoons dried oregano

2 tablespoons extra-virgin olive oil

Salt and ground white pepper

1 small head radicchio (red chicory), leaves separated

◼ Preheat an oven to 275°F (135°C).

◼ Wrap the fish in aluminum foil and place on a baking sheet in the center of the oven. Immediately reduce the heat to 225°F (105°C) and bake until warmed through, about 20 minutes. Remove from the oven and then from the foil.

◼ Transfer the fish to a cutting board and let cool briefly. Using a sharp knife, make 2 crosswise slashes, one below the gills and the other at the narrow part of the fish at the tail end, just until you reach the spine of the fish. Then, using the tip of the knife, make a lengthwise slash down the center of the fish, following the spine. Working from the center, lift off the skin and discard. Using the knife and a fork, lift one side of the fish fillet from the spine and transfer to a bowl. Lift the other side from the spine and transfer to the bowl. Turn the fish over and repeat with the other side. Flake the fish into bite-sized pieces.

◼ Slice each peeled orange crosswise into 3 thick rings. Cut each ring into small wedges by cutting between the membranes. Add to the bowl along with the olives, cheese, green onions, oregano and olive oil. Toss well. Season to taste with salt and white pepper.

◼ Place 1 or more radicchio leaves on each individual plate and top with an equal amount of the fish mixture. Serve at room temperature.

Serves 4

Bruschetta with Tomatoes, Beans and Fresh Herbs

In Tuscany, the city of Lucca is known for its outstanding olive oil, showcased here in the garlic-scented toast known as bruschetta. You can also serve the toasts topped with cured meats, marinated roasted peppers or other ingredients of your choosing.

TOPPING

1   cup (6 oz/185 g) seeded and diced ripe beefsteak tomato

¾   cup (5½ oz/170 g) well-drained cannellini beans (freshly cooked or canned)

¼   cup (1¼ oz/37 g) seeded and diced cucumber

2   tablespoons thinly sliced green (spring) onion

1   tablespoon fresh oregano leaves or 1½ teaspoons dried oregano

1   tablespoon chopped fresh basil or 1½ teaspoons dried basil

Freshly ground pepper

BRUSCHETTA

8   slices country-style white or whole-wheat (wholemeal) bread, each 2½ inches (6 cm) wide and ½ inch (12 mm) thick

1   large clove garlic, cut in half

4   teaspoons extra-virgin olive oil

◩ To make the topping, in a bowl, combine all the topping ingredients, including pepper to taste. Toss well, cover and refrigerate for at least 1–2 hours or for up to 2 days to allow the flavors to blend.

◩ To make the bruschetta, preheat a broiler (griller) or prepare a fire in a charcoal grill. Arrange the bread slices on a rack on a broiler pan or on a grill rack and broil or grill for 2 minutes. Turn the bread slices over and continue to cook until golden,

1–2 minutes longer. Remove from the heat, rub a cut side of the garlic clove over one side of each warm bread slice and then brush with ½ teaspoon of the olive oil.

◩ Mound an equal amount of the topping on the garlic-rubbed side of each bread slice. Transfer to a platter and serve immediately.

Serves 4

Grilled Shrimp Wrapped in Prosciutto and Zucchini

Assembled in advance, quickly cooked and accompanied by bruschetta, these marinated and skewered shrimp are excellent fare for a backyard barbecue. Shrimp, and their close cousins, scampi, are plentiful in the waters along Italy's lengthy coastline.

MARINADE
1	tablespoon fresh lemon juice
2	tablespoons fruity Italian white wine
2	tablespoons extra-virgin olive oil
8	lemon zest strips, each about 2 inches (5 cm) long
½	teaspoon crumbled bay leaf
1	teaspoon fresh thyme leaves or ½ teaspoon dried thyme
3	large cloves garlic, crushed Freshly ground pepper

SHRIMP SKEWERS
1	lb (500 g) jumbo shrimp (prawns), peeled and deveined (12–16 shrimp)
1	lb (500 g) zucchini (courgettes), trimmed and cut lengthwise into slices ⅛ inch (3 mm) thick (12–16 slices)
6–8	paper-thin slices prosciutto, cut lengthwise into halves

BRUSCHETTA
8	slices country-style white bread, each ½ inch (12 mm) thick
1	large clove garlic, cut in half
4	teaspoons extra-virgin olive oil Small fresh thyme sprigs

To make the marinade, in a shallow nonaluminum bowl, combine all the marinade ingredients, including pepper to taste, and stir until blended.

To make the shrimp skewers, add the shrimp to the marinade and turn to coat. Cover and refrigerate for at least 4 hours or as long as overnight.

Remove the shrimp from the refrigerator about 30 minutes before you cook them. Meanwhile, soak 4 bamboo skewers in water to cover.

Preheat a broiler (griller) or prepare a fire in a charcoal grill. Arrange the zucchini slices on a rack in a broiler pan or on a grill rack and broil or grill for 3 minutes. Turn the slices over and continue to cook until limp, 2–3 minutes longer. Set aside to cool. Leave the broiler on or maintain the charcoal fire.

Remove the shrimp from the marinade, reserving the lemon zest strips. Drain the skewers. Wrap 1 piece of prosciutto around the center of each shrimp, and then wrap with a zucchini slice. Thread 3 or 4 wrapped shrimp onto each skewer and then garnish each skewer with 2 of the reserved lemon strips.

Arrange the skewers on the rack of the broiler pan or on the grill rack over hot coals. Broil or grill the shrimp for 3–4 minutes. Turn the shrimp over and continue to cook until pink and slightly curled, 2–3 minutes longer.

While the shrimp cook, make the bruschetta. Toast or grill the bread, turning once, until golden on both sides. Rub a cut side of the garlic clove over one side of each warm bread slice, then brush with ½ teaspoon of the olive oil.

To serve, arrange the bruschetta and skewers on a platter or divide among individual plates. Garnish with the thyme sprigs and serve at once.

Serves 4

Country-Style Spinach Crostini

Crostini, among the most typical Italian antipasti, are prevalent in Tuscany, where toppings may range from warm sautéed Swiss chard to simple stewed beans. Here, sautéed spinach is topped with creamy melted cheese to form crusty gratinéed toasts.

2 tablespoons extra-virgin olive oil

3 tablespoons finely chopped prosciutto

2 tablespoons chopped green (spring) onions

1 lb (500 g) spinach, stems removed and chopped

1 large egg

2 tablespoons freshly grated good-quality Italian Parmesan cheese

1 tablespoon heavy (double) cream
Salt and ground white pepper
Freshly grated nutmeg

8 slices country-style white or whole-wheat (wholemeal) bread, each 2½ inches (6 cm) wide and ½ inch (12 mm) thick

2 oz (60 g) Swiss or Emmenthaler cheese, cut into 8 equal slices

▨ In a frying pan over medium heat, warm the olive oil. Add the prosciutto and green onions and sauté until fragrant, about 1 minute. Raise the heat to high, add the spinach and sauté until barely wilted, 2–3 minutes. Transfer to a colander to drain, pressing against the spinach with a spoon to remove any excess liquid. Let cool.

▨ Preheat a broiler (griller).

▨ In a bowl, whisk the egg until blended. Whisk in the Parmesan cheese and cream until well mixed. Season to taste with salt, white pepper and nutmeg. Add the spinach mixture and stir until blended.

▨ Toast the bread until golden. Using a slotted spoon to drain off any excess liquid, arrange the spinach mixture on top of the toasted bread slices, dividing it evenly and making sure all edges of the toasts are covered to prevent burning. Lay a slice of cheese on top of each toast. Place on a rack in a broiler pan and broil (grill) until the cheese has just melted, 1–2 minutes.

▨ Transfer to a platter and serve immediately.

Serves 4

Sicilian Eggplant and Zucchini Rollatini

*The use of currants and pine nuts in this specialty of Palermo reflects the exotic influences—
Greek, Middle Eastern, North African—that have helped to shape Sicilian cooking. Eggplant
appears on many trattoria menus, in everything from pastas to grilled-vegetable plates.*

1	large eggplant (aubergine), unpeeled
1	large zucchini (courgette)
3	tablespoons extra-virgin olive oil

STUFFING

⅔	cup (3 oz/90 g) dried bread crumbs
5	tablespoons (1¼ oz/37 g) chopped pine nuts
3	tablespoons dried currants
1½	oz (45 g) caciotta or provolone cheese, rind removed and chopped
3	tablespoons chopped fresh parsley
5	tablespoons (2 oz/60 g) diced Canadian bacon or smoked ham, optional
6	tablespoons (3 fl oz/90 ml) quick tomato sauce *(recipe on page 15)*
1	extra-large egg white, lightly beaten
	Salt and ground white pepper

TOPPING

1	cup (8 fl oz/250 ml) quick tomato sauce *(recipe on page 15)*
3	oz (90 g) caciotta or provolone cheese, rind removed and cut into 8 thin slices

◈ Preheat a broiler (griller). Slice the eggplant lengthwise into 8 slices each ¼ inch (6 mm) thick. Slice the zucchini lengthwise into 8 slices each ⅛ inch (3 mm) thick. Using about ¼ teaspoon of the olive oil for each side, lightly brush both sides of each eggplant and zucchini slice.

◈ Arrange the eggplant slices on a rack in a broiler pan and broil (grill) until barely cooked on one side, about 5 minutes. Turn the slices over and broil until lightly golden, 4–5 minutes longer. Remove from the broiler, transfer to a plate and let cool.

◈ Arrange the zucchini slices on the rack in the broiler pan and broil until barely cooked on one side, about 4 minutes. Turn the zucchini slices over and broil until just tender, 2–3 minutes longer. Remove the slices from the broiler, transfer to a plate and let cool.

◈ Position a rack in the middle of an oven and preheat to 400°F (200°C). Lightly brush the remaining olive oil over the bottom and sides of an 8-inch (20-cm) square nonmetal baking dish.

◈ To make the stuffing, in a bowl, stir together all the stuffing ingredients, including salt and white pepper to taste, until blended.

◈ To assemble the rollatini, on a clean work surface, lay 1 eggplant slice and place 1 zucchini slice on top of it. Using your fingertips, gently shape 2–3 tablespoons of the stuffing into a log and place in the center of the zucchini slice. Fold both ends of the eggplant and zucchini over the stuffing to cover fully, overlapping the ends. Place seam-side down in the prepared baking dish. Repeat with the remaining slices and stuffing.

◈ Cover the dish with aluminum foil and place in the center of the oven. Immediately reduce the heat to 350°F (180°C) and bake until heated through, 20–25 minutes.

◈ Spoon the tomato sauce evenly over the rolls and re-cover the dish. Bake until cooked through, 15–20 minutes. Divide the cheese slices evenly among the rollatini, placing them over the center of each roll. Bake, uncovered, until the cheese melts, 6–8 minutes.

◈ Remove from the oven and let stand for a few minutes. To serve, transfer 2 rolls to each warmed individual plate and serve immediately.

Serves 4

Stuffed Zucchini Flowers with Tomato-Mint Sauce

Gentle sautéing brings out the delightful peppery flavor of fresh zucchini flowers. In this simple preparation, the tender blossoms are filled with a sheep's milk cheese, then accented with a refreshing tomato-mint sauce. If you like, substitute mozzarella or Fontina for the caciotta or provolone.

16 zucchini (courgette) flowers, slightly closed

4 oz (125 g) caciotta or provolone cheese, rind removed

¼ cup (1½ oz/45 g) all-purpose (plain) flour

¼ cup (2 fl oz/60 ml) sunflower or safflower oil

TOMATO-MINT SAUCE

1 cup (8 fl oz/250 ml) quick tomato sauce *(recipe on page 15)*

2 large fresh mint leaves, thinly sliced, or ⅛ teaspoon dried mint

▣ Trim off the long stems from the flowers and carefully spread apart the petals slightly. Cut the cheese into 16 rectangles ½ inch (12 mm) wide by ½ inch (12 mm) thick by 1 inch (2.5 cm) long, or long enough to fit snugly inside the flowers. Insert 1 piece of cheese into each flower and close the petals over the cheese.

▣ Spread the flour on a plate. Gently roll each flower in the flour, carefully turning to coat lightly but evenly. Transfer to a plate.

▣ In a large frying pan over medium heat, warm the oil. When hot, add the stuffed flowers in a single layer and sauté for 2–3 minutes. Using 2 forks, carefully turn over the flowers and sauté until barely golden brown on the edges and the cheese has begun to melt, 1–2 minutes longer. The flowers should remain soft.

▣ Meanwhile, make the sauce. In a small saucepan over medium heat, warm the tomato sauce to a simmer. Add the mint and simmer for 1 minute longer.

▣ Using 2 forks, remove the flowers from the pan, draining any excess oil. Transfer to warmed individual plates, arranging 4 flowers on each plate with the stem ends toward the center. Spoon the tomato-mint sauce only over the stem end of each flower. Serve immediately.

Serves 4

Bocconcini Salad

Bite-sized balls of mozzarella, known as bocconcini, are ideal for making this colorful salad.
Look for them in Italian delicatessens, or cut larger mozzarella balls into small chunks. If possible,
seek out mozzarella di bufala, *made from water buffalo's milk; a specialty of central and*
southern Italy, it is a softer, creamier mozzarella than that made from cow's milk.

1 lb (500 g) mozzarella bocconcini
8 cherry tomatoes, cut in halves
½ cup (2½ oz/75 g) diced green bell pepper (capsicum)
½ cup (2½ oz/75 g) thickly sliced celery
½ cup (1½ oz/45 g) thickly sliced Belgian endive (chicory/witloof)
½ cup (1 oz/30 g) thickly sliced arugula (rocket)
1½ tablespoons fresh lemon juice
3 tablespoons extra-virgin olive oil
Salt and freshly ground pepper
2 tablespoons fresh basil leaves or 1 tablespoon dried basil

◼ In a large salad bowl, combine the mozzarella, cherry tomatoes, bell pepper, celery, endive and arugula.

◼ Pour the lemon juice into a small bowl. Gradually add the olive oil, pouring it in a slow, steady stream and whisking constantly until emulsified.

◼ Pour the mixture over the salad and season to taste with salt and pepper. Toss until all the ingredients are thoroughly coated with the dressing.

◼ Sprinkle the basil over the salad and serve immediately.

Serves 4

First Courses

The *primo piatto* is arguably the most recognizably Italian course of the trattoria meal, for this is when the grain dishes—the pasta, risotto and polenta—are served. Italians pride themselves particularly on their pasta, which has long been a daily staple. It has sustained them through hardships and poverty, and has become so integral to the national diet that it is often eaten twice a day. According to reliable sources, there are more than 100 different varieties of pasta served in Italy today.

Also popular as a first course in northern and central Italy are risottos, made by slowly cooking short-grained Arborio, Vialone Nano or Carnaroli rice in flavorful broths. Stone-ground corn in the form of polenta is served in these regions as well, where it might appear topped with a ragù of roasted vegetables.

Soups, listed on menus as *minestre,* likewise make excellent first courses. Great Italian soups range from a summertime blend of tomatoes and bread to a heartier concoction of pasta and beans. And for those days when you want a simpler meal, all of these *primi piatti* are well suited for serving as a light main course.

Lasagna Bolognese

In Italy, small portions of lasagna are customarily served as a first course, but this hearty dish would also make an excellent main dish for four. The combination of a creamy white sauce, Parmesan cheese and a rich meat sauce—ragù bolognese—is typical of Bologna.

1   recipe spinach pasta dough *(recipe on pages 12–13)*, or 1 lb (500 g) dried lasagne noodles

RAGÙ BOLOGNESE
3   tablespoons sunflower, safflower or canola oil
⅓   cup (2 oz/60 g) diced carrots
⅓   cup (2 oz/60 g) diced celery
⅓   cup (2 oz/60 g) diced yellow onion
6   oz (185 g) pancetta, coarsely ground (minced) or finely chopped
¾   lb (375 g) coarsely ground (minced) or finely chopped pork butt or shoulder
6   oz (185 g) coarsely ground (minced) or finely chopped veal
2   cans (28 oz/875 g each) plum (Roma) tomatoes, drained and chopped, plus juice from 1 can
    Salt and freshly ground pepper
    Freshly grated nutmeg

    White sauce *(recipe on page 36)*
    Ice water, as needed
½   lb (250 g) good-quality Parmesan cheese, freshly grated
    Salt and freshly ground pepper

◙ Make the spinach pasta dough, if using. Cover and let rest for 1 hour as directed, then roll out the dough about ¹⁄₁₆ inch (2 mm) thick. Cover with a damp cloth and set aside.

◙ To make the ragù, in a deep pot over low heat, warm the oil. Add the carrots and celery and sauté until the edges of the celery become translucent, about 5 minutes. Add the onion and sauté until almost translucent, about 5 minutes. Add the pancetta and cook, stirring occasionally, for 10 minutes. Then add the pork and veal and cook, stirring occasionally, until cooked but not browned, about 15 minutes. Add the tomatoes and juice and simmer, uncovered, stirring occasionally, until very thick, 2–2½ hours. Season to taste with salt, pepper and nutmeg.

◙ Cut the fresh pasta sheets, if using, into sixteen 4-by-10-inch (10-by-25-cm) strips. Prepare the white sauce and set aside.

◙ Fill a deep pot three-fourths full with salted water and bring to a rolling boil. Add the pasta all at once and gently stir to prevent the pasta from sticking together. Cook until not yet al dente, about 2 minutes for fresh pasta and 6 minutes for dried. Drain in a colander and immediately plunge the pasta into ice water to halt the cooking. Drain again and lay flat in a single layer on kitchen towels to dry briefly.

◙ Preheat an oven to 450°F (230°C). Select a 9-by-12-inch (23-by-30-cm) baking dish.

◙ Spread ½ cup (4 fl oz/125 ml) ragù over the bottom of the baking dish. Arrange a single layer of the pasta on top, being careful not to overlap. Spread ⅓ cup (2½ fl oz/80 ml) of the white sauce over the top and then top with another ½–⅔ cup (4–5 fl oz/125–160 ml) ragù. Sprinkle with 3–4 tablespoons of the Parmesan cheese, then season to taste with salt and pepper. Repeat with the pasta, sauces and cheese to make 7 pasta layers in all. Then arrange a final pasta layer on top and spread with only white sauce and cheese.

◙ Place in the center of the oven and immediately reduce the heat to 400°F (200°C). Bake until bubbling and golden brown, 35–45 minutes. Remove from oven and let stand for 5 minutes before cutting.

◙ To serve, cut into pieces and transfer to warmed individual plates.

Serves 8 as a first course, 4 as a main course

35

Cannelloni

The meat-and-ricotta filling for these filled pasta tubes can also be used to stuff ravioli, and the white sauce, known in Italian as besciamella, *may be replaced by quick tomato sauce (recipe on page 15). To simplify preparation further, use purchased pasta sheets.*

½ recipe basic egg pasta dough *(recipe on pages 12–13)* or 5 oz (155 g) purchased thin fresh pasta sheets

FILLING
2 teaspoons sunflower, safflower or canola oil
2 tablespoons minced yellow onion
¼ lb (125 g) ground (minced) pork shoulder or butt or ground veal
¼ lb (125 g) mortadella, ground (minced)
2 oz (60 g) prosciutto, ground (minced)
2 cups (1 lb/500 g) ricotta cheese
¾ cup (3 oz/90 g) freshly grated good-quality Parmesan cheese
Salt and ground white pepper
Freshly grated nutmeg

WHITE SAUCE
¼ cup (2 oz/60 g) unsalted butter
⅓ cup (2 oz/60 g) all-purpose (plain) flour
3 cups (24 fl oz/750 ml) milk, heated almost to a boil
Salt and ground white pepper
Freshly grated nutmeg

Ice water, as needed
½ cup (2 oz/60 g) freshly grated good-quality Parmesan cheese

▩ Make the basic pasta dough, if using. Cover with a bowl to prevent drying and set aside.

▩ To make the filling, in a small frying pan over medium heat, warm the oil. Add the onion and sauté until almost translucent, about 3 minutes. Add the pork or veal and simmer, stirring occasionally, for 5 minutes; do not allow to brown. Transfer to a colander to drain and let cool.

▩ In a bowl, combine the cooled meat mixture, mortadella, prosciutto and ricotta and Parmesan cheeses and mix well. Season to taste with salt, white pepper and nutmeg. Set aside.

▩ Roll out the basic pasta dough, if using, ⅟₁₆ inch (2 mm) thick. Cut the fresh or purchased sheets into eight 4½-inch (11.5-cm) squares. Set aside.

▩ To make the white sauce, in a saucepan over low heat, melt the butter. Whisk in the flour until blended, then gradually add the hot milk, whisking constantly. Simmer, whisking constantly and scraping the sides and bottom of the pan with a spatula as necessary to avoid burning, until the raw flour flavor dissipates, about 5 minutes. Remove from the heat and season to taste with salt, white pepper and nutmeg.

▩ Fill a deep pot three-fourths full with salted water and bring to a boil. Add the pasta all at once and stir gently to prevent sticking. Cook until not yet al dente, about 2 minutes. Drain, then plunge into ice water to halt the cooking. Drain again and lay flat in a single layer on kitchen towels to dry briefly.

▩ Preheat an oven to 450°F (230°C). Select a 9-by-12-inch (23-by-30-cm) baking dish. Spread 1 cup (8 fl oz/250 ml) of the white sauce over the bottom of the baking dish. To make the cannelloni, form about ⅓ cup (2 oz/60 g) of the filling into a log shape on the center of each pasta square and roll up into a cylinder. Place the rolls, seam side down, in a single layer in the dish. Evenly spread the remaining white sauce over the top. Sprinkle evenly with the cheese.

▩ Place in the center of the oven and immediately reduce the heat to 400°F (200°C). Bake until bubbling and golden brown on top, 30–35 minutes. Remove from oven and let stand for 5 minutes before serving.

▩ To serve, using a spatula, carefully transfer the cannelloni to warmed individual plates. Serve immediately.

Serves 8 as a first course, 4 as a main course

Pappardelle with Venison Ragù

Here, the venison is prepared in salmi, *marinated with herbs, spices and red wine. Although pappardelle traditionally has straight sides, a ruffled edge can be made with a fluted pastry wheel, if you wish.*

1   teaspoon fresh rosemary leaves
4   fresh sage leaves
2   bay leaves
1   cinnamon stick
1   teaspoon juniper berries
⅛   teaspoon whole cloves
1   lb (500 g) venison shoulder, cut into 1-inch (2.5-cm) cubes
1   celery stalk, quartered
1   carrot, peeled and quartered
1   yellow onion, quartered
1½ cups (12 fl oz/375 ml) red wine
½   recipe basic egg pasta dough *(recipe on pages 12–13)* or ½ lb (250 g) purchased fresh or dried pappardelle
1   tablespoon unsalted butter

RAGÙ
1   teaspoon fresh rosemary leaves
1   fresh sage leaf
1   bay leaf
1   cinnamon stick
1   tablespoon unsalted butter
¼   cup (1¼ oz/37 g) each diced yellow onion, carrot and celery
1   teaspoon minced garlic
1   cup (6 oz/185 g) peeled and chopped plum (Roma) tomatoes
½   cup (4 fl oz/125 ml) red wine
2   tablespoons dry Marsala wine
2½ cups (20 fl oz/625 ml) meat stock *(recipe on page 14)*
2   tablespoons unsalted butter, melted

☒ Place the rosemary, sage, bay leaves, cinnamon stick, juniper berries and cloves on a square of cheesecloth (muslin), bring the corners together and tie with kitchen string. In a shallow nonaluminum bowl, combine the venison, celery, carrot, onion, wine and cheesecloth bag. Cover and refrigerate overnight.

☒ The next day, make the basic pasta dough, if using. Divide the dough into 2 pieces, one twice as large as the other. Shape the large piece into a ball, cover with a bowl to prevent drying and set aside; reserve the smaller piece for another use.

☒ Remove the venison from the marinade, discarding the marinade. In a deep pot over high heat, melt the butter. Add the venison and brown on all sides, about 10 minutes. Transfer the meat to a plate and set the meat and the pot aside.

☒ To make the ragù, place the rosemary, sage, bay leaf and cinnamon stick on a square of cheesecloth and tie securely with kitchen string. In the same pot, melt the butter over medium heat. Add the onion, carrot and celery and sauté until the onion and celery are translucent, about 5 minutes. Add the garlic, cheesecloth bag and tomatoes and sauté for 2 minutes. Add the venison and red wine and cook for 2 minutes.

☒ Add the Marsala and continue to cook for 1 minute longer. Add the stock and bring to a boil over high heat. Reduce the heat to low and simmer, uncovered, until the venison is tender when pierced and about 2 cups (16 fl oz/500 ml) liquid remains, 45–55 minutes.

☒ Meanwhile, roll out the basic pasta dough, if using, ⅟₁₆ inch (2 mm) thick. Cut into noodles ¾ inch (2 cm) wide. Gather loosely into small piles; set aside to dry for at least 30 minutes.

☒ When the sauce is ready, using a slotted spoon, remove the venison; set aside. Discard the cheesecloth bag. Ladle the vegetables into a food processor and purée. Return to the pot over low heat, bring to a simmer and simmer for 5 minutes. Add the venison and simmer until the sauce is thick, about 15 minutes.

☒ Meanwhile, fill another deep pot three-fourths full with salted water and bring to a boil. Add the pasta all at once and stir gently. Cook until al dente, 2–3 minutes for fresh pasta and 6–8 minutes for dried. Drain briefly in a colander, then immediately transfer to a serving bowl.

☒ Add the melted butter and toss well. Add the venison ragù and toss again. Serve immediately.

Serves 4

Orecchiette with Broccoli Rabe, Garlic and Pine Nuts

A variety of small, round pasta shaped like little ears, orecchiette are typically found in southern Italian trattorias, especially those in Apulia. Broccoli rabe has longer stems, smaller flower heads and a somewhat more bitter flavor than regular broccoli, which can be substituted.

1	lb (500 g) broccoli rabe
¾	lb (375 g) dried orecchiette
1	tablespoon unsalted butter
2	tablespoons extra-virgin olive oil
½	cup (2½ oz/75 g) finely chopped yellow onion
½	cup (2½ oz/75 g) pine nuts
1–2	fresh small red chilies, seeded and sliced into thin rings
4	teaspoons chopped garlic
1½	cups (12 fl oz/375 ml) vegetable or meat stock *(recipes on pages 14–15)*
2	tablespoons chopped fresh parsley
1	cup (1 oz/30 g) fresh cilantro leaves (fresh coriander), optional
	Salt and freshly ground pepper
	Freshly grated good-quality Italian Parmesan or pecorino romano cheese

◻ Trim any tough portions from the broccoli rabe, then cut the stems and leaves into 1-inch (2.5-cm) lengths; leave the florets whole. Place the stems on a steamer rack over (not touching) gently boiling water; cover and steam for 2–3 minutes. Add the leaves and florets and steam until cooked through yet firm when pierced with a fork, 2–3 minutes longer. Remove from the rack and set aside.

◻ Fill a deep pot three-fourths full with salted water and bring to a rolling boil. Add the pasta and stir gently to prevent the pasta from sticking together. Cook until al dente, 10–12 minutes or according to package directions.

◻ Meanwhile, in a large frying pan over medium heat, melt the butter with the olive oil. Add the onion and pine nuts and sauté until the onion is translucent and the pine nuts are lightly golden, about 3 minutes; do not allow the onion to brown. Add the chilies and garlic and sauté for a few seconds until very fragrant. Add the broccoli rabe and sauté for 2 minutes. Add the stock, bring to a boil, then reduce the heat to low and simmer for 1 minute.

◻ Drain the orecchiette briefly in a colander and immediately add it to the frying pan. Toss well. Add the parsley and cilantro, if using, and toss well again. Season to taste with salt and pepper.

◻ Transfer to a warmed serving bowl and sprinkle with the cheese. Serve immediately.

Serves 4

Penne with Arugula in Tomato-Cream Sauce

*Combining tomato sauce with cream produces a delicate-looking rose-colored sauce whose
mild, sweet flavor complements the slight saltiness of prosciutto and the pleasant pepperiness of arugula.
Other tubular pastas, such as rigatoni, can be used in place of the penne.*

3 oz (90 g) prosciutto, finely diced

1¾ cups (14 fl oz/440 ml) quick tomato sauce *(recipe on page 15)*

1 cup (8 fl oz/250 ml) heavy (double) cream

3 oz (90 g) arugula (rocket), stems removed and chopped
Salt and ground white pepper

1 lb (500 g) dried penne

◙ In a saucepan over medium heat, combine the prosciutto and tomato sauce. Bring to a simmer and simmer for 3–4 minutes. Pour in the cream, stir until blended and simmer for 1 minute. Add the arugula and cook just until wilted, about 1 minute longer. Season to taste with salt and white pepper.

◙ Meanwhile, fill a deep pot three-fourths full with salted water and bring to a rolling boil. Add the pasta and stir gently to prevent the pasta from sticking together. Cook until al dente, 8–10 minutes or according to package directions. Drain the pasta briefly in a colander and immediately add it to the saucepan. Stir to mix well, coating the pasta with the sauce.

◙ Transfer to a warmed serving platter or individual bowls and serve immediately.

Serves 4

43

Eggplant and Walnut Ravioli in Tomato-Pesto Sauce

Combine Genoa's signature pesto sauce with tomato sauce and you create pesto corto, *which tops these eggplant-stuffed ravioli and is also good on the region's local pasta ribbons,* trenette.

FILLING

1   large eggplant (aubergine), peeled and cut crosswise into slices ½ inch (12 mm) thick

¼   cup (1 oz/30 g) walnuts, finely chopped

1   cup (8 oz/250 g) ricotta cheese

¼   cup (1 oz/30 g) freshly grated good-quality Parmesan cheese

4   teaspoons minced fresh parsley

2   tablespoons minced fresh basil

1   tablespoon minced fresh sage
    Salt and ground white pepper

1   recipe basic egg pasta dough *(recipe on pages 12–13)* or ¾ lb (375 g) purchased thin fresh pasta sheets

TOMATO-PESTO SAUCE

½   cup (½ oz/15 g) firmly packed fresh basil leaves

1½   teaspoons pine nuts

1   teaspoon finely chopped walnuts

1   clove garlic

3   tablespoons freshly grated Italian Parmesan cheese

⅓   cup (3 fl oz/80 ml) extra-virgin olive oil
    Salt and ground white pepper

1   tablespoon unsalted butter

¾   cup (6 fl oz/180 ml) quick tomato sauce *(recipe on page 15)*

1   wedge, 2 oz (60 g) Italian Parmesan cheese

◉ To make the filling, preheat a broiler (griller). Arrange the eggplant slices on a rack in a broiler pan and broil (grill) until lightly browned, 3–4 minutes. Turn the slices over and broil (grill) on the second side until lightly browned and tender, 2–3 minutes.

◉ Transfer the eggplant to a cutting board and cut into small pieces; you should have about 1 cup (8 oz/250 g). Place on kitchen towels to drain off any excess liquid and let cool.

◉ In a food processor fitted with the metal blade or in a blender, combine the eggplant, walnuts and ¼ cup (2 oz/60 g) of the ricotta cheese and purée until smooth. Transfer to a bowl and add the remaining ricotta and Parmesan cheeses, parsley, basil and sage and stir until blended. Cover and refrigerate for at least a few hours or for up to 1 day before using. Just before using, season to taste with salt and white pepper.

◉ Meanwhile, make the basic pasta dough, if using. Cover and let rest for 1 hour as directed, then roll out the dough ⅛ inch (3 mm) thick.

◉ Using a cookie cutter 2½ inches (6 cm) in diameter, cut out 64 disks from the fresh or purchased pasta sheets. Cover the disks with a damp kitchen towel to prevent drying; re-serve any remaining pasta for another use. Place 1 teaspoon filling in the center of a disk, brush the edges of the disk with a little water, and top with a second disk. Gently press the edges together, sealing well. Place in a single layer on a rack until slightly dry to the touch, 1–2 hours.

◉ Meanwhile, make the pesto for the sauce. In a food processor fitted with the metal blade, purée the basil, pine nuts, walnuts and garlic. Add the cheese and blend well. With the processor on, pour in the oil in a steady stream until thick. Season to taste with salt and pepper.

◉ Fill a deep pot three-fourths full with salted water and bring to a rolling boil. Add the ravioli all at once. Gently stir to prevent sticking. Boil until al dente, 3–4 minutes.

◉ Meanwhile, in a large frying pan over medium heat, melt the butter and stir in the tomato sauce. Just before the ravioli are done, stir in the reserved pesto sauce.

◉ Drain the ravioli briefly in a colander and immediately add to the sauce. Stir gently to coat and arrange on warmed individual plates.

◉ Using a small, sharp knife or a vegetable peeler, shave thin slices from the Parmesan wedge and sprinkle over the ravioli. Serve at once.

Serves 8 as a first course, 4 as a main course

Genoa Pansotti with Artichokes

Along the Ligurian coast on the Gulf of Genoa in northwestern Italy, herbs grow in profusion. They add their distinctive fragrance to a wealth of local fish and pasta dishes, including these pansotti cloaked with an herb-laced butter sauce. Spinach or watercress may be substituted for the arugula.

FILLING

2   oz (60 g) steamed fresh artichoke hearts *(see glossary, page 124)* or thawed, frozen artichoke hearts

¼   cup (2 oz/60 g) ricotta cheese

2   tablespoons mascarpone cheese

½   cup (2 oz/60 g) freshly grated good-quality Italian Parmesan cheese

1   teaspoon minced arugula (rocket)

1   teaspoon minced fresh parsley

¼   teaspoon minced garlic
    Salt and ground white pepper
    Freshly grated nutmeg

½   recipe basic egg pasta dough *(recipe on pages 12–13)* or ½ lb (250 g) purchased thin fresh pasta sheets

SAUCE

¼   cup (2 oz/60 g) unsalted butter

½   cup (2½ oz/75 g) chopped steamed fresh artichoke hearts *(see glossary, page 124)* or thawed, frozen artichoke hearts

2   tablespoons chopped fresh parsley, basil, thyme, marjoram, sage or chives, or a mixture

¼   cup (½ oz/15 g) thinly sliced arugula (rocket)
    Salt and ground white pepper

◩ To make the filling, in a blender or in a food processor fitted with the metal blade, combine the artichokes and ricotta cheese and purée until smooth. In a bowl, combine the artichoke mixture, mascarpone and Parmesan cheeses, arugula, parsley and garlic. Using a spoon, stir until very smooth. Cover and refrigerate for at least 2 hours or for up to 1 day. Just before using, season to taste with salt, white pepper and nutmeg.

◩ Make the basic pasta dough, if using. Cover and let rest for 1 hour as directed, then roll out the dough ⅛ inch (3 mm) thick.

◩ Cut the fresh or purchased pasta into forty-eight 2-inch (5-cm) squares. Cover the squares with a damp kitchen towel to prevent them from drying; reserve any remaining pasta for another use. Place about ½ teaspoon filling in the center of each square. Brush the edges of the square with a little water and fold each square in half, forming a triangle and covering the filling completely. Stretch the pasta, if necessary, so the points of the triangle meet. Gently press the edges together, sealing well. Place in a single layer on a rack until slightly dry to the touch, 1–2 hours.

◩ Fill a deep pot three-fourths full with salted water and bring to a rolling boil. Add the pansotti all at once. Gently stir to prevent the pansotti from sticking together. Boil until al dente, 2–3 minutes.

◩ Meanwhile, make the sauce. In a large frying pan over low heat, melt the butter. Add the chopped artichoke hearts and sauté until heated through, about 1 minute. Drain the pasta briefly in a colander and immediately add it to the artichokes. Raise the heat to high and toss the pasta gently. Add the herbs and arugula and toss again until mixed.

◩ Season to taste with salt and white pepper. Transfer to warmed plates and serve immediately.

Serves 8 as a first course, 4 as a main course

Tagliatelle with Seafood, Sun-Dried Tomatoes and Olives

*Tagliatelle, a classic pasta of Bologna and the surrounding Emilia-Romagna region,
forms a delicate bed for a sauce of quickly sautéed seafood from the Adriatic coast. Fettuccine,
generally thicker and slightly narrower than tagliatelle, may be substituted.*

1   recipe basic egg pasta dough *(recipe on pages 12–13)* or 1 lb (500 g) purchased fresh or dried fettuccine

SAUCE

1   tablespoon unsalted butter

2   tablespoons minced shallots

2   cups (16 fl oz/500 ml) heavy (double) cream

¼   cup (2 fl oz/60 ml) dry Italian white wine

6   oz (185 g) medium shrimp (prawns), peeled, deveined and cut in halves lengthwise

¼   lb (125 g) sea scallops, sliced crosswise ¼ inch (6 mm) thick

½   cup (4 oz/125 g) oil-packed sun-dried tomatoes, drained and cut into thin julienne strips

½   cup (3 oz/90 g) oil-cured black olives, pitted and cut in halves

½   cup (2 oz/60 g) freshly grated good-quality Italian Parmesan cheese
    Salt and ground white pepper
    Freshly grated nutmeg

▦ Make the basic pasta dough, if using. Cover and let rest for 1 hour as directed, then roll out the dough about 1/16 inch (2 mm) thick. Cut into noodles ¼ inch (6 mm) wide. Separate the pasta strands and toss gently to prevent sticking. Set aside to dry for at least 30 minutes.

▦ To make the sauce, in a large frying pan over medium heat, melt the butter. Add the shallots and sauté until almost translucent, about 3 minutes. Pour in the cream and bring to a boil. Reduce the heat to medium and simmer, uncovered, until slightly thickened, about 6 minutes. Add the wine and simmer for 1 minute.

▦ Meanwhile, fill a deep pot three-fourths full with salted water and bring to a rolling boil. Add the pasta all at once. Gently stir to prevent the pasta from sticking together. Boil until al dente, 2–3 minutes for fresh pasta and 6–8 minutes for dried or according to package directions.

▦ While the pasta is cooking, add the shrimp, scallops and sun-dried tomatoes to the sauce and simmer for 1 minute. Add the olives and Parmesan cheese. Raise the heat to high and bring to a boil.

▦ Drain the pasta briefly in a colander and immediately add it to the sauce. Toss well and cook briefly until the pasta is very hot.

▦ Season to taste with salt, white pepper and nutmeg. Transfer to warmed individual plates and serve immediately.

Serves 4

Spinach Gnocchi in Gorgonzola Cream Sauce

*On northern Italian trattoria tables during winter, you'll frequently find these little dumplings
served as a warming, satisfying first course. For the lightest gnocchi, use yellow-fleshed potatoes such as
Yukon Gold or Finnish Yellow; white-fleshed potatoes produce denser, but no less delicious, results.*

SPINACH GNOCCHI

1¼ lb (625 g) fresh spinach, stems removed, or 1 package (10 oz/ 315 g) thawed, frozen leaf spinach

26 oz (815 g) yellow- or white-fleshed potatoes *(see note)*, unpeeled, cut into large pieces

2½ cups (12½ oz/390 g) all-purpose (plain) flour, plus ½ cup (2½ oz/ 75 g) flour for dusting

1 extra-large egg

GORGONZOLA SAUCE

2 cups (16 fl oz/500 ml) heavy (double) cream

2 oz (60 g) sweet Gorgonzola cheese, crumbled

3 tablespoons fruity Italian white wine

1 teaspoon Cognac or other brandy, optional
Salt and ground white pepper
Freshly grated nutmeg

◩ To make the gnocchi, if using fresh spinach, place the spinach on a steamer rack over (not touching) boiling water. Cover and steam until wilted and tender, 3–4 minutes. Transfer the steamer rack holding the spinach to a sink to drain and let cool.

◩ Using your hands, gather the cooled or thawed, frozen spinach into a ball; squeeze out any excess moisture. In a food processor fitted with the metal blade, purée the spinach until smooth. Transfer to paper towels, squeeze to remove any remaining moisture and set aside.

◩ Place the potatoes on a steamer rack over (not touching) boiling water, cover and steam until tender, 8–10 minutes. Remove the potatoes from the steamer rack. While still hot, peel the potatoes, then pass them through a ricer onto a clean work surface, forming a broad, low mound. Sprinkle the 2½ cups (12½ oz/390 g) flour on top and quickly and gently "fluff" the potato and flour together with your fingertips.

◩ Place the puréed spinach on top and, using a fork or your fingertips, begin to work it into the potato and flour mixture to form a dough. Place the egg on top and lightly mix it in. Press the dough together, then knead just until a dough forms.

◩ Scrape the work surface clean. Sprinkle a little more flour on the work surface. Divide the dough into 6 equal portions; cover 5 of the portions with a kitchen towel to prevent drying. Form the sixth portion into a log ¾ inch (2 cm) in diameter. Cut crosswise into pieces ¾ inch (2 cm) wide. If the pieces are sticky, lightly coat them with some of the remaining flour. Repeat with the remaining 5 portions.

◩ Fill a deep pot three-fourths full with salted water and bring to a rolling boil. Add the gnocchi all at once. Gently stir to prevent the gnocchi from sticking together. Boil until just cooked through, 12–15 minutes.

◩ Meanwhile, make the Gorgonzola sauce. In a frying pan over high heat, bring the cream to a boil. Boil until slightly thickened, about 4 minutes. Stir in the cheese and reduce the heat to medium. Stir in the wine and simmer for 1 minute. Stir in the brandy, if using. Season to taste with salt, white pepper and nutmeg.

◩ Drain the gnocchi and immediately add them to the sauce. Toss well to coat. Spoon onto warmed individual plates and serve immediately.

Serves 8 as a first course, 4 as a main course

Risotto with Saffron

In Lombardy and the Piedmont, short-grained rice varieties such as Arborio, Vialone Nano and Carnaroli are grown specifically for making risotto. If you like, prepare the risotto partially in advance and finish the cooking about 15 minutes before serving.

3 tablespoons unsalted butter

2 tablespoons minced shallots

1 cup (7 oz/220 g) rice *(see note)*

2½ cups (20 fl oz/625 ml) meat or vegetable stock *(recipes on pages 14–15)*, or as needed, heated

½ cup (4 fl oz/125 ml) dry Italian white wine, plus white wine to taste

Generous pinch of powdered saffron (one 125-mg packet), optional

¼ cup (1 oz/30 g) freshly grated good-quality Italian Parmesan cheese, or to taste

Salt and ground white pepper

Freshly grated nutmeg

In a deep saucepan over low heat, melt 2 tablespoons of the butter. Add the shallots and sauté until almost translucent, about 2 minutes. Stir in the rice, coating it thoroughly with the butter. Cook, stirring, until the edges of the grains are translucent, about 2 minutes.

Add 1 cup (8 fl oz/250 ml) of the stock and simmer over medium heat, stirring occasionally, until the rice absorbs most of the stock and there is only a little visible liquid remaining, 5–6 minutes.

Add another 1 cup (8 fl oz/250 ml) stock, stir to mix and again allow the rice to absorb most of the liquid, another 5–6 minutes. (At this point, you can remove the risotto from the heat and set aside for up to 2 hours.)

Reduce the heat to medium-low, add the ½ cup (4 fl oz/125 ml) wine and saffron and stir to distribute the saffron evenly. Allow the rice to absorb most of the wine, stirring

occasionally to prevent sticking. Add another ½ cup (4 fl oz/125 ml) stock and continue to simmer, stirring, for 4–5 minutes.

Stir in the Parmesan cheese, the remaining 1 tablespoon butter and season to taste with salt, white pepper and nutmeg. The risotto should be al dente at this point. If it is too moist, simmer for a few minutes longer; if it is too dry, stir in a little additional stock to achieve the desired consistency. Taste and adjust with more wine, cheese and seasonings.

Remove from the heat when there is a little more liquid than the desired amount, as the rice will continue to absorb it. To serve, mound the risotto in warmed shallow bowls and serve immediately.

Serves 4

Seafood Risotto

*Laden with fresh mussels, shrimp and scallops, creamy rice and seafood stews like this
one abound in the trattorias of Italy's coastal villages. To serve as a generous main dish,
double all of the ingredients and increase the cooking time by about 10 minutes.*

MUSSELS
1   tablespoon olive oil
1   tablespoon minced shallots
1   tablespoon minced garlic
½   cup (4 fl oz/125 ml) dry
    Italian white wine
48 mussels in the shell, beards
    removed and scrubbed

RISOTTO
2   tablespoons unsalted butter
2   tablespoons minced shallots
1   teaspoon minced garlic
1   cup (7 oz/220 g) Vialone Nano,
    Arborio or Carnaroli rice
1¾ cups (14 fl oz/440 ml) fish
    stock *(recipe on page 14),* or as
    needed, heated
⅔   cup (5 fl oz/160 ml) dry
    Italian white wine
4   small dried chilies, optional
1   cup (6 oz/185 g) peeled, seeded
    and chopped ripe plum (Roma)
    tomatoes (fresh or canned)
¼   lb (125 g) shrimp (prawns),
    peeled, deveined and chopped
¼   lb (125 g) sea or bay scallops,
    chopped
    Salt and ground white pepper
2   teaspoons chopped fresh parsley

◩ To prepare the mussels, in a large frying pan over medium heat, warm the olive oil. Add the shallots and garlic and sauté for 1 minute. Pour in the wine and add the mussels, discarding any that do not close to the touch. Cover, raise the heat to high, and cook until the mussels open, 3–4 minutes. Remove from the heat and discard any mussels that did not open.

◩ Transfer 32 mussels in their shells to a bowl; cover to keep warm. Remove and discard the shells from the remaining mussels, cover and set aside separately. Strain the broth through a fine-mesh sieve lined with cheesecloth (muslin) into another bowl; set aside.

◩ To make the risotto, in a deep saucepan over low heat, melt the butter. Add the shallots and garlic and sauté until the shallots are almost translucent, about 2 minutes. Stir in the rice and cook, stirring, until the edges of the grains are translucent, about 2 minutes. Add enough fish stock to the mussel broth to make 2½–3 cups (20–24 fl oz/625–750 ml).

◩ Add 1 cup (8 fl oz/250 ml) of the broth mixture to the rice and simmer over medium heat, stirring occasionally, until only a little visible liquid remains, 5–6 minutes. Stir in another ½ cup (4 fl oz/125 ml) of the broth

mixture and again allow the rice to absorb most of the liquid, another 3–4 minutes.

◩ Add ½ cup (4 fl oz/125 ml) of the wine and the chilies, if using, and simmer over low heat, stirring occasionally, for 3–4 minutes. Stir in the tomatoes and simmer for 3 minutes. Add another 1 cup (8 fl oz/250 ml) broth mixture and simmer, stirring occasionally, for 5 minutes. Stir in the shrimp, scallops and shelled mussels and simmer for 2 minutes.

◩ Stir in the remaining wine. Season to taste with salt and white pepper. The risotto should be al dente at this point. If it is too moist, simmer for a few minutes longer; if it is too dry, stir in a little additional stock to achieve the proper consistency. Remove and discard the chilies. Taste and adjust the seasoning.

◩ Remove from the heat when there is still a little more liquid than desired, as the rice will continue to absorb it. Mound in warmed shallow bowls and surround each serving with 8 mussels. Sprinkle with the parsley and serve immediately.

Serves 4

Polenta with Roasted Vegetable Ragù

Creamy cooked polenta is a popular primo piatto. *You can also cook the polenta as directed, spread it on a baking sheet to a thickness of about ½ inch (12 mm) and let cool until set. Then cut it into 3-inch (7.5-cm) squares, bake, broil or fry until heated through and serve as a side dish or with a savory topping.*

ROASTED VEGETABLE RAGÙ

1 small butternut (pumpkin) squash, cut in half and seeds removed
1 small turnip, parsnip or rutabaga (swede), peeled and quartered
1 small zucchini (courgette), quartered
1 small eggplant (aubergine), peeled and quartered lengthwise
1 small green bell pepper (capsicum), halved and seeded
4 ripe tomatoes, about 1 lb (500 g)
1 leek, cut in half lengthwise and carefully washed
3 oz (90 g) fresh white mushrooms
2 tablespoons olive oil
1 cup (8 fl oz/250 ml) vegetable or meat stock *(recipes on pages 14–15)*
2 tablespoons dry white wine
Salt and ground black pepper

POLENTA

4 cups (32 fl oz/1 l) water
2 tablespoons unsalted butter
1 cup (5 oz/155 g) coarse-grind polenta (quick-cooking or regular)
3 tablespoons fresh herbs, such as oregano, thyme and/or marjoram, or 1½ tablespoons dried herbs
¾ cup (3 oz/90 g) freshly grated good-quality Italian Parmesan cheese
Salt and ground white pepper

▨ To roast the vegetables for the ragù, preheat an oven to 450°F (230°C). Put the butternut squash in a baking pan and place in the center of the oven. Bake, uncovered, until soft but not mushy when pierced, about 1 hour.

▨ About 40 minutes before the squash is ready, place all the other vegetables in a large baking pan, keeping each vegetable separate, and cover with aluminum foil. Place the second baking pan in the oven and bake for 15–20 minutes. Uncover and continue to bake until tender when pierced with a fork, 20–25 minutes longer. Remove all the vegetables from the oven and let cool.

▨ Peel the butternut squash. Cut the squash; turnip, parsnip or rutabaga; zucchini; eggplant; bell pepper and tomatoes into ½-inch (12-mm) dice. Thinly slice the leek crosswise, and quarter the mushrooms. Keep the vegetables separate.

▨ To make the ragù, in a saucepan over medium heat, warm the olive oil. Add the turnip, parsnip or rutabaga and leek and sauté for 1 minute. Raise the heat to high and add the zucchini, eggplant, bell pepper and mushrooms and sauté for 2 minutes. Add the squash and sauté for 1 minute. Add the tomatoes and sauté for 1 minute longer. Add the stock and bring to a boil, then reduce the heat to medium and simmer until the flavors are blended, 2–3 minutes. Add the wine and simmer for 1 minute longer. Season to taste with salt and black pepper. Keep warm.

▨ To make the polenta, in a deep saucepan over high heat, bring the water and butter to a boil. Slowly pour in the polenta while stirring continuously with a whisk. Allow the mixture to bubble, whisking constantly, for 1–2 minutes as it thickens. Reduce the heat to low and continue to simmer, whisking constantly to prevent burning and lumps from forming, until the polenta grains swell and are tender like porridge, about 5 minutes for quick-cooking polenta and 20 minutes for regular polenta or according to package directions. During the last few minutes of cooking, stir in the herbs and cheese and season to taste with salt and white pepper.

▨ Ladle the polenta onto warmed individual plates. Make a well in the center of each serving, ladle the ragù over the top and serve.

Serves 4

Four Seasons Pizza

Arguably the most popular pizza in Italy, the quattro stagioni *pie represents the four seasons in its use of toppings: artichokes for spring, olives for summer, mushrooms for autumn and prosciutto for winter.*

PIZZA DOUGH
2   teaspoons active dry yeast
⅔   cup (5 fl oz/160 ml) warm water, 105°–115°F (40°–46°C)
¼   teaspoon sugar
2   cups (10 oz/315 g) unbleached all-purpose (plain) flour, plus flour for dusting
    Salt and ground white pepper
1   tablespoon extra-virgin olive oil

PIZZA SAUCE
1   cup (8 fl oz/250 ml) quick tomato sauce (*recipe on page 15*) or purchased tomato sauce
2   teaspoons minced garlic
2   teaspoons fresh oregano leaves
1   tablespoon fresh basil leaves

    Cornmeal or semolina

TOPPING
2   tablespoons freshly grated good-quality Italian Parmesan cheese
3   oz (90 g) mozzarella cheese, thinly sliced
3   oz (90 g) smoked mozzarella cheese, thinly sliced
4   thin slices prosciutto or baked ham, halved lengthwise
4–8 fresh shiitake, cremini or white mushrooms, stems removed and brushed clean
6   oil-cured black olives, pitted and cut in halves
4   artichoke hearts, quartered lengthwise (drained, canned or thawed, frozen)

◙ To make the pizza dough, in a small bowl, stir together the yeast, warm water and sugar and let stand until foamy, about 5 minutes.

◙ Place the 2 cups (10 oz/315 g) flour and salt and white pepper to taste in a mixing bowl or in a food processor fitted with the metal blade. Add the oil, then the yeast mixture while stirring or processing continuously until the mixture begins to gather into a ball.

◙ Transfer the dough to a lightly floured work surface and knead a few times until the dough feels smooth. Form into a ball and place in a bowl. Cover the bowl tightly with plastic wrap and let the dough rise in a warm place until doubled, about 1½ hours.

◙ To make the pizza sauce, make ½ recipe (1 cup/8 fl oz/250 ml) quick tomato sauce, if using, adding the garlic, oregano and basil as directed. Set aside to cool. If using purchased tomato sauce, pour the sauce into a small saucepan and bring to a boil. Add the garlic, oregano and basil, reduce the heat to low and simmer for 2 minutes. Set aside to cool.

◙ Sprinkle some cornmeal or semolina on a rimless baking sheet. Place the dough on the sheet and, using your fingertips, press and stretch the dough into a round 12 inches (30 cm) in diameter, forming a slight rim at

the dough edge. Cover with a kitchen towel and let rise again in a warm place until tripled in height, about 1½ hours.

◙ Place a pizza stone, if you have one, on the middle rack of an oven and preheat to 475°F (245°C).

◙ Using a fork, pierce the dough in even intervals to allow steam to escape during cooking. Spread the tomato sauce over the dough round. Then, for the topping, scatter the Parmesan evenly over the sauce. Place the mozzarella cheeses in an even layer over the Parmesan cheese. Arrange the prosciutto, mushrooms, olives and artichokes on top, overlapping them with the cheeses.

◙ Place the pizza in the center of the oven or, if you are using a pizza stone, slide the pizza from the sheet onto the stone. Immediately reduce the oven temperature to 425°F (220°C) and bake until the dough is cooked and the cheese is light golden brown, 25–30 minutes. Remove the pizza from the oven and let stand for a few minutes before serving.

◙ To serve, slice into wedges and transfer to individual plates.

Serves 4

Tuscan Vegetable Soup

The addition of a grain imparts body and rich, earthy flavor to this hearty country soup. Spelt, an ancient variety of wheat known in Italy as farro, *is highly prized in Tuscany for its pleasantly nutty flavor and slightly crunchy texture. Look for it in well-stocked Italian shops or health-food stores.*

1	cup (7 oz/220 g) spelt, barley or long-grain white rice
4–5	cups (32–40 fl oz/1–1.25 l) water
2	broccoli stalks
1	small leek, white part only
1	small celery stalk
1	large carrot, peeled
2	tablespoons extra-virgin olive oil, plus olive oil for garnish
1	cup (4 oz/125 g) chopped yellow onion
1½	cups (9 oz/280 g) peeled, seeded and chopped plum (Roma) tomatoes (fresh or canned)
½	cup (2½ oz/75 g) peeled and thinly sliced white turnip
5	cups (40 fl oz/1.25 l) vegetable or meat stock *(recipes on pages 14–15)*
¾	cup (3½ oz/105 g) diagonally sliced green beans
1	small zucchini (courgette), cut in half lengthwise, then thinly sliced crosswise
	Salt and freshly ground pepper
	Freshly grated good-quality Italian Parmesan cheese

In a bowl, combine the spelt, barley or rice and 3 cups (24 fl oz/750 ml) of the water. Let stand for 1 hour.

Meanwhile, cut the broccoli, leek, celery and carrot into slices ¼ inch (6 mm) thick; set aside.

In a soup pot over low heat, warm the 2 tablespoons olive oil. Add the onion and sauté until translucent, about 5 minutes. Add the tomatoes and sauté for 2 minutes. Drain the spelt, barley or rice and add it to the pot, along with the turnip, broccoli, leek, celery and carrot. Cook, stirring, for 3 minutes.

Add the stock and another 1 cup (8 fl oz/250 ml) of the water. Bring to a boil, reduce the heat to low, cover and simmer for 15 minutes.

Add the green beans and zucchini, cover, and continue to simmer, stirring occasionally, until the vegetables are soft yet retain their shape and the grain is tender, 35–40 minutes. If the soup becomes too thick, stir in the remaining 1 cup (8 fl oz/250 ml) water. Season to taste with salt and pepper.

To serve, ladle the soup into warmed individual soup bowls. Lace each serving with a thin drizzle of olive oil and sprinkle the cheese on top. Serve immediately.

Serves 4

Summer Tomato-Bread Soup

*When summer's tomatoes are at their peak, Florentine trattorias combine them with stale bread
and fruity olive oil to make this seasonal soup. To capture the true Italian character of this rustic dish,
use a dense country-style white, whole-wheat (wholemeal) or mild brown loaf.*

1	lb (500 g) country-style bread *(see note)*
3	tablespoons extra-virgin olive oil, plus olive oil for garnish
2	small cloves garlic, thinly sliced
5–5½	lb (2.5–2.75 kg) ripe plum (Roma) or beefsteak tomatoes, peeled, seeded and chopped (7 cups/2⅔ lb/1.3 kg)
1	fresh sage leaf, minced
½	teaspoon minced fresh basil
	Salt and freshly ground pepper
3–4	cups (24–32 fl oz/750 ml–1 l) vegetable or meat stock *(recipes on pages 14–15)*
2	teaspoons red wine vinegar

Trim off the crusts from the bread and cut the bread into 1-inch (2.5-cm) cubes; you should have about ½ lb (250 g). Place in a single layer on a tray and let dry, uncovered, overnight.

In a deep, heavy-bottomed soup pot over low heat, warm the 3 tablespoons olive oil. Add the garlic and sauté until fragrant but not brown, about 1 minute. Add the bread and sauté for 2 minutes; do not allow to brown. Add the tomatoes and cook, stirring occasionally, until they begin to soften, about 5 minutes. Add the sage and basil and season to taste with salt and pepper.

As the bread absorbs the tomatoes, add some of the stock as needed to keep the mixture soupy. At the same time, use a spoon to mash the bread so the soup is thick and the bread blends into the tomato sauce.

Cook the soup, stirring occasionally to prevent burning, until thickened and no chunks of bread remain, 30–40 minutes. Remove from the heat and let rest for 30–60 minutes to allow the flavors to blend and develop.

Return the pot to low heat and stir in the vinegar. Bring to a simmer and simmer until the sharp fumes of the vinegar have evaporated, about 1 minute. Taste and adjust the seasoning.

To serve, ladle into warmed individual bowls and lightly drizzle olive oil on top.

Serves 4

Main Courses

The classic Italian meal builds to *il secondo piatto,* the main course. Literally translated as "the second plate," it follows gracefully on the heels of the more delicate *primo piatto* and is often accented with the full range of Mediterranean flavors—herbs, tomatoes, garlic, olives, capers and lemon.

During much of the year, poultry, meat and fish are rather simply prepared for this course, generally grilled, broiled or sautéed to preserve their fresh tastes and enticing aromas. In the winter, however, robust roasts, stews and braised dishes are more common fare. These are usually served family style in generous portions on platters or in bowls that are set in the center of the table for everyone to share. Grains and vegetables are traditionally offered on the side.

A variation is the *piatto unico,* or meal-in-one-dish: a balanced union of meat or fish and vegetables on a single plate. The southern Italian specialty of veal chops topped with bitter greens typifies such a preparation. Contemporary Italian cooking, in which swordfish rolls might conceal small caches of shrimp, has greatly expanded the repertoire of trattoria main courses.

Braised Veal Shanks with Lemon, Parsley and Garlic

Outside of Italy, ossobuco *often lacks its distinctive topping of* gremolata, *a heady mixture of lemon zest, garlic and parsley. Offer polenta (recipe on page 56) instead of the risotto, if you like, and don't overlook the marrow concealed within the veal bones; spread it on toast for a delectable finale.*

VEAL SHANKS

½ cup (2½ oz/75 g) unbleached all-purpose (plain) flour

4 veal shanks, about 4 lb (2 kg) total weight, each about 2 inches (5 cm) thick

2 tablespoons unsalted butter

2 tablespoons extra-virgin olive oil

½ cup (2½ oz/75 g) chopped yellow onion

½ cup (2½ oz/75 g) peeled, diced carrot

½ cup (2½ oz/75 g) diced celery

⅓ cup (2 oz/60 g) diced fennel

1 teaspoon minced garlic

2 teaspoons fresh marjoram leaves

2 teaspoons fresh thyme leaves

1 bay leaf

1¼ cups (8 oz/250 g) peeled, seeded and chopped tomatoes

1 cup (8 fl oz/250 ml) dry Italian white wine

2–3 cups (16–24 fl oz/500–750 ml) meat stock *(recipe on page 14)*
Salt and freshly ground pepper

Risotto with saffron *(recipe on page 53)*

GREMOLATA

½ cup (¾ oz/20 g) chopped fresh Italian (flat-leaf) parsley

1½ teaspoons minced lemon zest

½ teaspoon minced garlic

◪ To prepare the veal shanks, spread the flour on a plate and evenly coat the veal shanks with the flour, shaking off any excess.

◪ In a large frying pan or pot over medium-high heat, melt the butter with the olive oil. When hot, add the veal shanks and lightly brown on both sides, about 4 minutes per side. Remove the veal shanks from the pan and set aside.

◪ Reduce the heat to medium-low and add the onion, carrot, celery and fennel. Sauté until the edges of the onion are translucent, 3–4 minutes; do not allow to brown. Add the garlic, marjoram, thyme and bay leaf and stir until blended. Add the tomatoes and bring to a boil. Return the veal to the pan and cook for 1 minute. Raise the heat to high, pour in the wine and deglaze the pan by stirring to dislodge any browned bits from the pan bottom.

◪ When the mixture boils, add about 2 cups (16 fl oz/500 ml) of the stock; the liquid should reach three-fourths of the way up the sides of the veal shanks. Reduce the heat to medium-low, cover partially and simmer, turning the shanks over occasionally. Continue cooking, adding more stock as needed to keep the mixture moist,

until the veal is tender when pierced with a fork and there are about 2 cups (16 fl oz/500 ml) of liquid and vegetables remaining, about 2½ hours. If there is too much liquid, uncover and boil gently to concentrate the broth. Season to taste with salt and pepper.

◪ While the stew is cooking, make the risotto. Just before serving, make the *gremolata* by tossing together the parsley, lemon zest and garlic in a small bowl until evenly mixed.

◪ To serve, discard the bay leaf. Place a mound of risotto on each individual plate. Place 1 veal shank on top of each mound of risotto. Spoon the broth and vegetables on top. Sprinkle with the *gremolata* and serve immediately.

Serves 4

Neapolitan-Style Braised Beef Braciole

A favorite dish in the trattorias of central and southern Italy is tender braciole, beef slices concealing a filling of cheese and vegetables. Open a good Chianti or other robust red wine both for cooking and enjoying with the meal.

1   lb (500 g) top beef round, cut into 4 thin slices

¼   lb (125 g) smoked baked ham, cut into 4 thin slices

¼   lb (125 g) provolone cheese, cut into 4 thin slices

2   tablespoons chopped fresh parsley

4   teaspoons minced garlic

3   tablespoons chopped, peeled carrot

4   teaspoons plus 2 tablespoons chopped celery

3   tablespoons extra-virgin olive oil

¼   cup (1½ oz/45 g) chopped red (Spanish) onion

½   cup (4 fl oz/125 ml) plus 2 tablespoons Italian red wine (*see note*)

2   cans (28 oz/875 g each) plum (Roma) tomatoes, drained and puréed (3½ cups/28 fl oz/875 ml purée)
    Salt and freshly ground pepper

◎ Place each beef slice between 2 sheets of plastic wrap and, using a meat pounder, pound until ⅛ inch (3 mm) thick. Place 1 ham slice on top of each beef slice, and then top with a cheese slice.

◎ In a small bowl, mix together the parsley, 2 teaspoons of the garlic, 1 tablespoon of the carrot and the 4 teaspoons celery. Sprinkle the mixture evenly over the center of each cheese slice. Beginning at one end of each beef slice, tightly roll up and secure the seam with toothpicks. Seal the ends with toothpicks as well, to keep the filling from spilling out.

◎ In a deep saucepan over medium heat, warm the olive oil. Add the beef rolls and brown well on all sides, 4–5 minutes. Reduce the heat to medium-low, add the remaining 2 tablespoons carrot, 2 tablespoons celery and the onion and sauté for 2 minutes. Add the remaining 2 teaspoons garlic and sauté until fragrant, 1–2 minutes.

◎ Raise the heat to high, add the ½ cup (4 fl oz/125 ml) red wine and deglaze the pan by stirring to dislodge the browned bits from the pan bottom. Boil for 1 minute, then add the tomato purée. Return to a boil, then reduce the heat to low and simmer, uncovered, until the beef is tender when pierced with a fork, about 1½ hours.

◎ Add the remaining 2 tablespoons red wine and continue to simmer for 2 minutes longer. Season to taste with salt and pepper. Spoon onto warmed individual plates, remove the toothpicks, and serve immediately.

Serves 4

Roman Roast Lamb with Rosemary and Garlic

The appearance of roast lamb on trattoria menus, especially around Rome, traditionally signals the coming of spring. Cooking lamb in this manner yields especially tender, succulent results. To make carving easier, ask your butcher to crack the bones between the ribs.

2   racks of lamb, 8 chops per rack and about 4 lb (2 kg) total weight, cracked
¼   cup (2 fl oz/60 ml) sunflower or canola oil
    Small fresh rosemary sprigs
    Garlic cloves, cut into quarters lengthwise
2   cups (16 fl oz/500 ml) full-bodied Italian white wine, or as needed
    Freshly ground pepper
    Salt
    Lemon wedges

▨ Using a sharp knife, score the fat on the top surface of the lamb to prevent curling and shrinking. In a large frying pan over high heat, warm the oil. When hot, add a lamb rack and brown on all sides, about 5 minutes. Place the rack, bone side down, in a large roasting pan. Repeat with the other rack.

▨ Preheat an oven to 450°F (230°C). Place rosemary and garlic between the chops, pushing them to the bottom where the bones are cracked and using whatever amount suits your taste. Stud the scored surface with rosemary and garlic as well. Pour white wine over the chops into the pan to a depth of ¼ inch (6 mm) and grind pepper over the racks.

▨ Place in the center of the oven, immediately reduce the heat to 400°F (200°C) and roast, basting once with the wine, until golden brown, about 1 hour.

▨ Remove the pan from the oven, baste the lamb again with the wine and cover with aluminum foil. Return to the oven and continue to roast for 20 minutes. Remove the foil, baste again, and continue to roast the lamb, uncovered, until the surface is deep brown and crisp, about 10 minutes longer.

▨ Transfer the lamb to a cutting board and let stand for 15 minutes before carving. If the lamb becomes cool, warm in a 225°F (105°C) oven for 2–3 minutes just before carving.

▨ Carve into chops and distribute among warmed individual plates. Season to taste with salt and pepper and garnish with lemon wedges.

Serves 4

Grilled Veal Chops with Salad

Nothing could be more rustic and elegant at the same time: a succulent veal chop straight from the charcoal grill, topped with an assortment of fresh bitter greens and thinly sliced artichokes. The meat juices marry superbly with the greens, forming the ideal trattoria piatto unico, or "meal in one dish."

VEAL CHOPS
- 4 veal loin chops with bone, ½ lb (250 g) each
- 2 cloves garlic, cut in halves lengthwise
  Freshly ground pepper
- 4 teaspoons extra-virgin olive oil

SALAD
- 1 small bunch arugula (rocket), stems removed
- 2 radicchio (red chicory) leaves, sliced into thin shreds
- 4 Belgian endive (chicory/witloof) leaves, sliced into thin shreds
- 2 small artichokes, trimmed (raw or thawed, frozen), optional
- 1 wedge, 1 oz (30 g), good-quality Italian Parmesan cheese

- 4 lemon wedges
  Extra-virgin olive oil

◙ To prepare the veal chops, using a sharp knife, slash the fat along the edge of each chop in 3 places to avoid curling during cooking. Place each chop between 2 sheets of plastic wrap and, using a meat pounder, pound ½ inch (12 mm) thick. Rub each chop all over with half of a garlic clove, pepper to taste and 1 teaspoon of the olive oil. Let stand at room temperature for 1 hour.

◙ Preheat a broiler (griller) or prepare a fire in a charcoal grill.

◙ Arrange the chops on a rack in a broiler pan or place on a grill rack over hot coals. Broil or grill, turning once, until done to your liking. For rare, cook 2–3 minutes on the first side and 1–2 minutes on the second; for medium, cook 4–5 minutes on the first side and 3–4 minutes on the second; for well-done, cook 6–7 minutes on the first side and 5–6 minutes on the second.

◙ Transfer the chops to warmed individual plates and scatter an equal amount of arugula, radicchio and endive over the top of each chop. Thinly slice the artichokes lengthwise, if using, and scatter over the salad. Using a sharp knife or vegetable peeler, shave off paper-thin slices of the Parmesan and scatter over the greens. Place a lemon wedge on each plate and pass the olive oil for drizzling over the top.

Serves 4

Broiled Chicken with Oregano, Lemon and Olives

This Mediterranean-inspired dish offers a wonderfully fragrant and subtly spicy way to serve broiled chicken. Because it is best served at room temperature, you can make it up to 1 hour in advance and serve as an al fresco dish for a picnic. If you like, substitute fresh rosemary leaves for the oregano.

1   chicken, 4 lb (2 kg)

MARINADE
2   tablespoons extra-virgin olive oil
2   tablespoons dry Italian white wine
6   large cloves garlic, crushed
4–6 teaspoons fresh oregano leaves or 2–3 teaspoons dried oregano
     Red pepper flakes or small whole red chilies (fresh or dried)

GARNISH
     Fresh oregano sprigs
     Zest from 1 lemon, cut into thin julienne strips
12   oil-cured black olives
12   cracked Sicilian green olives
     Red pepper flakes or small whole red chili peppers (fresh or dried)
     Salt

◙ Cut the chicken into 10 serving pieces.

◙ To make the marinade, in a large nonaluminum dish, combine all the marinade ingredients, including red pepper flakes or chilies to taste. Stir well, then add the chicken pieces. Toss to coat evenly, then cover and refrigerate for a few hours or as long as overnight. Remove from the refrigerator 1 hour before cooking.

◙ Preheat a broiler (griller) or prepare a fire in a charcoal grill.

◙ Place the chicken pieces, skin side down, on a rack in a broiler pan or on a grill rack over hot coals. Broil or grill until golden around the edges, 20–22 minutes. Turn the chicken over and continue to cook until golden brown around the edges on the second side and opaque throughout when cut with a knife, about 20 minutes longer.

◙ Transfer the chicken to a large serving platter and garnish with oregano sprigs, lemon zest, black and green olives and red pepper flakes or chilies to taste. Let rest for at least 30 minutes, to blend the flavors. Season to taste with salt and serve at room temperature.

Serves 4

Stuffed Chicken Breasts in Mushroom~Wine Sauce

To make these easier to fill and roll, select the broadest chicken breasts you can find. Slices
of turkey or veal can also be used for making this dish. If you like, you can assemble the rolls up to
2 hours in advance, cover and refrigerate, then flour and cook just before serving.

FILLING

2   teaspoons unsalted butter
2   tablespoons finely chopped
    yellow onion
1   teaspoon minced garlic
¾   lb (375 g) spinach, stems
    removed and chopped
3   tablespoons drained and chopped,
    oil-packed sun-dried tomatoes
2   tablespoons freshly grated good-
    quality Italian Parmesan cheese
    Salt and ground white pepper

4   skinless, boneless chicken breast
    halves, about ¼ lb (125 g) each
4   thin slices Emmenthaler cheese
2   tablespoons canola oil
½   cup (2½ oz/75 g) all–purpose
    (plain) flour

MUSHROOM-WINE SAUCE

2   teaspoons unsalted butter
⅛   cup (½ oz/15 g) thinly sliced
    yellow onion
½   lb (250 g) fresh white mushrooms,
    stems removed and thinly sliced
¼   cup (2 fl oz/60 ml) fruity Italian
    white wine
½   cup (4 fl oz/125 ml) meat or vege-
    table stock *(recipes on pages 14–15)*
¼   cup (2 fl oz/60 ml) heavy
    (double) cream
    Salt, ground white pepper and
    freshly grated nutmeg

To make the filling, in a frying pan over medium heat, melt the butter. Add the onion and sauté for 1 minute. Raise the heat to medium-high, add the garlic and spinach and sauté until the spinach is wilted, 2–3 minutes. Stir in the sun-dried tomatoes. Transfer the spinach mixture to a colander and, using the back of a wooden spoon, press gently against the mixture to remove any excess moisture, then let cool. Wipe the frying pan clean and set aside.

Transfer the spinach mixture to a bowl. Stir in the Parmesan cheese and season to taste with salt and white pepper. Set aside.

Place each chicken breast between 2 sheets of plastic wrap and, using a meat pounder, pound until ¼ inch (6 mm) thick. Place 1 cheese slice on top of each pounded breast. Spoon one-fourth of the spinach filling onto the bottom center of each cheese slice and shape the filling into a log, being careful that it does not protrude over the edges. Fold the sides in toward the center and then, beginning at the bottom end, roll up tightly. Secure with toothpicks.

Preheat an oven to 425°F (220°C). In the frying pan over medium-high heat, warm the oil. While the oil is heating, spread the flour on a plate.

Roll the stuffed chicken breasts in the flour, coating lightly and evenly. Add the chicken to the pan and brown lightly on all sides, 5–7 minutes.

Using a slotted spatula, transfer the chicken to a baking dish. Place in the center of the oven and immediately reduce the heat to 375°F (190°C). Bake until cooked through, 10–12 minutes. Transfer to warmed individual plates and let stand for a few minutes. Remove the toothpicks.

While the chicken is baking, make the mushroom-wine sauce. In a small frying pan over medium heat, melt the butter. Add the onion and sauté until the edges begin to turn translucent, about 2 minutes. Add the mushrooms and sauté until barely limp, about 2 minutes. Pour in the wine and deglaze the pan by stirring to dislodge any browned bits from the pan bottom. Cook over medium heat until the wine is reduced by half, about 2 minutes. Add the stock and simmer until reduced by half, 3–4 minutes. Pour in the cream and simmer until the sauce thickens slightly, 1–2 minutes. Season to taste with salt, white pepper and nutmeg.

Spoon the sauce over the chicken and serve immediately.

Serves 4

77

Cornish Hens with Roasted Vegetables

In Italy, this fragrant dish would be made with a faraona *(guinea hen), a species first brought to the country from Africa at the time of the Roman Empire when it was known as a Carthaginian or Numidian chicken. Try to find a young balsamic vinegar, aged only about five years, for the marinade.*

2   fresh Cornish hens (spatchcocks), 3–4 lb (1.5–2 kg) total weight

MARINADE
⅓   cup (3 fl oz/80 ml) extra-virgin olive oil
½   cup (4 fl oz/125 ml) balsamic vinegar
1   tablespoon chopped garlic
3   tablespoons chopped shallots
4   teaspoons fresh rosemary leaves or 2 teaspoons dried rosemary
15   fresh sage leaves or 1 teaspoon ground dried sage
2   bay leaves
    Freshly ground pepper

VEGETABLES
2   large broccoli florets
2   large cauliflower florets
1   zucchini (courgette)
1   whole head garlic
2   yellow onions, cut in halves
1   cup (8 fl oz/250 ml) water, or as needed

◈ Cut each hen in half. To make the marinade, in a shallow nonaluminum dish, combine all the marinade ingredients, including pepper to taste. Place the hens in the marinade, turning to coat evenly. Cover and refrigerate overnight, turning once.

◈ To prepare the vegetables, preheat an oven to 450°F (230°C). Cut the broccoli and cauliflower florets lengthwise into smaller florets each about 2–3 inches (5–7.5 cm) in diameter. Cut the zucchini in half lengthwise and then cut in half crosswise to make quarters. Remove some outside layers of papery skin from the head of garlic and cut off the top one-fourth of the head, exposing the cloves.

◈ Arrange all the vegetables, including the onions, in the bottom of a deep roasting pan. Pour in the water to a depth of ⅛ inch (3 mm). Cover with aluminum foil. Place the pan in the center of the oven and immediately reduce the heat to 400°F (200°C). Roast for 15 minutes.

◈ Remove the pan from the oven, remove the foil and rest a flat roasting rack on the edges of the pan over (not touching) the vegetables. Remove the hens from the marinade,

reserving the marinade, and place the hen halves on the rack, skin side down. Place in the center of the oven and continue roasting for 45 minutes.

◈ Remove the pan from the oven and drain off any excess water, leaving ⅛ inch (3 mm) in the bottom of the pan. Turn the vegetables over, and then turn the hen halves over, skin side up, and baste with the reserved marinade.

◈ Continue to roast until the hens are a deep brown and cooked through when cut with a knife and the vegetables are tender, about 30 minutes. (Check the vegetables during the last 15 minutes of roasting and remove them from the oven if done to your liking.)

◈ Remove the hens from the oven and let stand for 10 minutes. To serve, transfer to warmed individual plates, dividing the hens and vegetables evenly among them.

Serves 4

Duck with Vin Santo

Vin Santo, Italy's popular sherrylike wine, reputedly got its name in Florence around 1440, when Cardinal Bessarione sipped it at a banquet and declared, "Ma questo è un vino santo"—"Now there is a holy wine!" This dish can be served in two courses, with the sauce—thinned with 1 cup (8 fl oz/250 ml) meat stock—spooned over fettuccine as a first course, followed by the braised duckling pieces.

1	White Pekin or Long Island duckling, 5 lb (2.5 kg), preferably with giblets
2	tablespoons extra-virgin olive oil
¾	cup (4 oz/125 g) peeled, diced carrot
¾	cup (4 oz/125 g) diced celery
½	cup (4 fl oz/125 ml) water, or as needed
¾	cup (4 oz/125 g) diced yellow onion
3	oz (90 g) lean prosciutto, trimmed of fat and chopped
1	teaspoon minced garlic
2	fresh sage leaves or ¼ teaspoon dried sage
1	teaspoon fresh thyme leaves or ½ teaspoon dried thyme
1	teaspoon fresh marjoram leaves or ½ teaspoon dried marjoram
1	teaspoon fresh rosemary leaves or ½ teaspoon dried rosemary
½	bay leaf
1⅔	cups (13 fl oz/410 ml) Vin Santo
2½	cups (20 fl oz/625 ml) meat stock *(recipe on page 14)*

◻ Set the duck giblets aside, if included. Cut the duckling into 12 serving pieces. In a 5-qt (5-l) pot over medium-high heat, warm the olive oil. Add the duckling and brown evenly on all sides, 10–12 minutes. Transfer the duckling to a plate and pour off all but 1 tablespoon of the fat and oil from the pot.

◻ In the same pot over medium heat, add the carrot and celery and sauté, stirring occasionally and adding a little of the water as needed to prevent burning, until the edges of the celery begin to turn translucent, about 5 minutes. Add the onion and prosciutto and sauté, stirring occasionally and adding more water as needed to prevent burning, until the vegetables are barely soft but not browned, about 4 minutes.

◻ Return the duckling to the pan, along with the giblets, if using, the garlic, sage, thyme, marjoram, rosemary and bay leaf. Raise the heat to high, add the Vin Santo and deglaze the pan by stirring to dislodge any browned bits from the pan bottom.

Bring to a boil, reduce the heat to low, cover partially and simmer, stirring occasionally, for 15 minutes.

◻ Turn the duckling pieces over, add the stock and continue to simmer, partially covered, until the duckling is tender and there are about 2 cups (16 fl oz/500 ml) sauce remaining, about 2 hours. Remove the bay leaf and the giblets.

◻ To serve, skim off any fat from the surface and spoon the duckling and sauce into warmed individual serving dishes. Serve immediately.

Serves 4

Mediterranean Scallop Stew with Crostini

Scallops are harvested in abundance from the waters of the northern Adriatic Sea. In this dish, they are combined with the flavors of orange, fennel and herbs. Like many of the classic Italian seafood stews, this one is spooned over garlic-scented toasts known as crostini before serving.

1½   lb (750 g) bay or sea scallops

2   tablespoons extra-virgin olive oil, plus extra for brushing on bread

1⅓   cups (4 oz/125 g) sliced leeks, white part only

½   cup (2 oz/60 g) thinly sliced yellow onion

6   oz (185 g) pancetta, trimmed of fat and cut into thin strips

4   cloves garlic, thinly sliced, plus 1 clove garlic, cut in half

2   cups (12 oz/375) peeled, seeded and chopped plum (Roma) tomatoes (fresh or canned)

1½   cups (12 fl oz/375 ml) fruity Italian white wine

5   cups (40 fl oz/1.25 l) fish stock *(recipe on page 14)*

½   pound fresh white mushrooms, stems removed and sliced

4   tablespoons chopped fresh parsley

1   bay leaf

2   orange zest strips, each 2 inches (5 cm) long and ½ inch (12 mm) wide

½   teaspoon fresh thyme leaves

¼   teaspoon fennel seeds

⅛   teaspoon powdered saffron
       Salt and ground white pepper

4   slices country-style white bread
       Small fresh basil leaves
       Freshly grated good-quality Italian Parmesan cheese

❑ If using sea scallops, cut crosswise into slices ½ inch (12 mm) thick. Set aside.

❑ In a large saucepan or stockpot over medium heat, warm the 2 tablespoons olive oil. Add the leeks and onion and sauté until barely translucent, about 3 minutes; do not allow to brown. Add the pancetta and sauté for about 2 minutes to blend the flavors. Add the sliced garlic and tomatoes and sauté for 1 minute.

❑ Raise the heat to high, add 1¼ cups (10 fl oz/310 ml) of the wine and deglaze the pan by stirring to dislodge any browned bits from the pan bottom. Bring to a boil and add the stock, mushrooms, parsley, bay leaf, orange zest, thyme, fennel seeds and saffron. Return to a boil, then reduce the heat to medium and simmer, uncovered, for 15–20 minutes, to blend the flavors.

❑ Add the scallops and cook until not quite opaque in the center, 2–3 minutes. Add the remaining ¼ cup (2 fl oz/60 ml) wine and simmer until the scallops are just opaque throughout, about 1 minute longer. Remove the bay leaf and season to taste with salt and pepper.

❑ Meanwhile, toast the bread slices until golden. Rub a cut side of the halved garlic clove over one side of each warm bread slice and then brush with olive oil to taste.

❑ To serve, place 1 bread slice, garlic-rubbed side up, in the bottom of each of 4 warmed individual bowls. Ladle the stew over the bread slices. Garnish with the basil leaves and Parmesan cheese and serve immediately.

Serves 4

Swordfish Rolls Stuffed with Shrimp

Nearly any seaside trattoria in Sicily would be likely to have some variation of this skewered specialty on its menu. The skewers may be either baked, broiled or grilled.

4   boneless swordfish steaks, about 6 oz (185 g) each and ¾ inch (2 cm) thick

SHRIMP FILLING
¼   lb (125 g) shrimp (prawns)
¼   cup (1 oz/30 g) pine nuts
¼   cup (1 oz/30 g) freshly grated pecorino romano cheese
⅔   cup (3 oz/90 g) dried bread crumbs
2   tablespoons minced yellow onion
1   teaspoon minced garlic
2   teaspoons capers, rinsed
2   tablespoons chopped fresh parsley
⅓   cup (1 oz/30 g) chopped fresh white mushrooms
2   tablespoons white wine
2   teaspoons chopped fresh oregano
3   tablespoons chopped fresh basil
1   large egg, lightly beaten
    Salt and ground white pepper

1   cup (4 oz/125 g) dried bread crumbs
½   cup (4 fl oz/125 ml) olive oil
12   bay leaves
1   cup (3½ oz/105 g) sliced yellow onion
3   cups (12 oz/375 g) sliced yellow squash or zucchini
1   cup (4 oz/125 g) sliced green bell pepper (capsicum)
¼   cup (2 fl oz/60 ml) white wine
8   oil-cured black olives, pitted
    Salt and ground white pepper
    Lemon wedges

◻ Place 4 bamboo skewers in water to cover and let soak for about 30 minutes. Remove the skin from the swordfish steaks and discard. Place each steak between 2 sheets of plastic wrap and, using a meat pounder, pound ¼ inch (6 mm) thick. Then cut each piece in half to make 8 pieces in all. Set aside.

◻ To make the filling, peel and devein the shrimp. Chop the shrimp and pine nuts and place them in a bowl. Add all the remaining filling ingredients, including salt and pepper to taste. Stir until well blended.

◻ Place an equal portion of the filling in the center of each swordfish piece and gently shape it into a log; do not allow the filling to protrude over the edges of the fish. Roll up the swordfish to enclose the filling.

◻ Spread the bread crumbs on a plate. Brush the swordfish rolls with ¼ cup (2 fl oz/60 ml) of the olive oil and then coat evenly with the bread crumbs. Drain the skewers and thread 2 rolls on each skewer, placing a bay leaf between each roll and a bay leaf on either end as well.

◻ If baking the rolls, place the skewers in a baking pan. Preheat an oven to 450°F (230°C). Place the pan in the center of the oven and immediately reduce the heat to 400°F (200°C). Bake for 12 minutes. Turn over the rolls and continue to bake until the fish is opaque throughout, 12–14 minutes longer.

◻ If broiling or grilling the rolls, preheat a broiler (griller) or prepare a fire in a charcoal grill. Place on a rack in a broiler pan or on a grill rack over hot coals and cook as directed for baked rolls.

◻ In a frying pan over medium heat, warm the remaining olive oil. Add the onion and sauté until fragrant, about 1 minute. Add the squash or zucchini and sauté until almost tender when pierced, 3–4 minutes; do not brown and add a little water if needed to prevent sticking. Stir in the bell pepper and sauté for 1 minute. Raise the heat to high, add the wine and boil until the wine is reduced by half and the vegetables are tender but not mushy, 2–3 minutes. Stir in the olives and salt and white pepper to taste.

◻ To serve, spoon the vegetables onto warmed individual plates and arrange the skewered rolls and a lemon wedge alongside. Serve hot.

Serves 4

Monkfish with Potatoes and Artichokes

Italian country cooks recognize the natural affinity between potatoes and artichokes, a marriage that is enhanced here by the mild sweetness of fennel and the mellow richness of monkfish. For the monkfish, you can substitute medallions of halibut, baby cod or haddock, or slices of mahi-mahi fillet.

4   small artichokes, trimmed
    (see glossary, page 124)
4   new potatoes
1½   lb (750 g) monkfish fillets
2   tablespoons unsalted butter
1   tablespoon extra-virgin olive oil
¼   cup (2 fl oz/60 ml) dry Italian white wine
2   tablespoons minced shallots
2   teaspoons thinly sliced garlic
⅓   cup (2 oz/60 g) diced fennel
4   ripe plum (Roma) tomatoes, peeled, seeded and cut into ½-inch (12-mm) dice
½   cup (4 fl oz/125 ml) fish stock *(recipe on page 14)*
    Salt and ground white pepper

◻ Place the trimmed artichokes and potatoes on a steamer rack over (not touching) boiling water. Cover and steam until tender when pierced with a fork, 5–7 minutes for the artichokes and 8–10 minutes for the potatoes. Remove the vegetables from the steamer rack. When cool enough to handle, cut the artichokes lengthwise into quarters; peel the potatoes and cut crosswise into slices ¼ inch (6 mm) thick.

◻ Preheat an oven to 225°F (105°C).

◻ Trim off any thick outer membrane of the monkfish and cut into medallions ½ inch (12 mm) thick. At the top of each individual plate, arrange 6–8 potato slices in a fan, overlapping them slightly. Place 4 artichoke quarters in a fan below them, overlapping the potatoes. Keep warm in the oven.

◻ In a large frying pan over medium-high heat, melt the butter with the olive oil. When the pan is hot, add the monkfish and cook until white on the first side, about 1 minute. Turn the monkfish over and cook for 1 minute longer. Pour in the wine,

reduce the heat to medium, cover and simmer until the monkfish is just cooked through and tender, 2–3 minutes; do not overcook or the monkfish will become chewy. Remove the pan from the heat and transfer the monkfish to the plates, arranging the medallions at the base of the artichoke fan. Place in the warm oven.

◻ In the same pan over medium heat, add the shallots and garlic and sauté until fragrant, just a few seconds. Add the fennel and sauté for 1 minute. Raise the heat to high, add the tomatoes and sauté for 1 minute longer. Pour in the stock and cook over medium heat until reduced by one-third, or until the sauce thickens slightly and the fennel is cooked yet slightly firm, 2–3 minutes.

◻ Remove the sauce from the heat, season to taste with the salt and white pepper and spoon over the monkfish, artichokes and potatoes. Serve immediately.

Serves 4

Side Dishes

Vegetables are a traditional part of every Italian meal. They appear, usually combined with other ingredients, in the *antipasti, primi* and *secondi,* but they assume their proper status when listed under their own menu category of *contorni.* From these choices on the trattoria menu, diners order vegetables to accompany their main dishes.

Trattoria chefs employ simple cooking methods—roasting, baking, sautéing—to produce a wealth of classic vegetable dishes year-round. The featured ingredients usually represent the best the market has to offer that day, so little embellishment is needed to bring out the full, rich flavors. Vegetables are often cooked with a touch of onion, garlic and herbs and perhaps a light lacing of butter, olive oil or wine, so that the finished dish enhances rather than overwhelms the main-course selection.

While every region in Italy emphasizes its own special preparations for locally grown produce, fresh vegetables are universally appreciated. Sometimes a *contorno* even becomes the main dish. During the heat of summer, or when the main meal is eaten at lunchtime, Italians find a plate of cooked vegetables refreshingly restorative at the end of the day.

Oven-Roasted Potatoes with Rosemary and Garlic

All over Italy, trattorias prepare potatoes in this simple manner. For the best flavor, select yellow-fleshed potatoes such as Finnish Yellow or Yukon Gold, or white-fleshed Maine potatoes. Serve the potatoes with Roman roast lamb with rosemary and garlic (recipe on page 70), grilled veal chops with salad (page 73) or Cornish hens with roasted vegetables (page 78).

¼ cup (2 fl oz/60 ml) extra-virgin olive oil

12 large cloves garlic, lightly crushed

1½ lb (750 g) yellow-fleshed potatoes, peeled and cut into 1-inch (2.5-cm) pieces

8 fresh rosemary sprigs, or to taste
Salt and freshly ground pepper

▣ Preheat an oven to 425°F (220°C).

▣ In a metal baking pan over low heat, warm the olive oil and the garlic until the oil is hot and garlic flavor is released into the oil, 1–2 minutes. Remove from the heat.

▣ Meanwhile, fill a saucepan three-fourths full with water and bring to a boil. Place the potatoes in the boiling water for 10 seconds, then drain and immediately transfer the potatoes to the baking pan holding the garlic and oil, leaving a little water still dripping from the potatoes. (This step helps to prevent the potatoes from breaking during roasting.)

▣ Sprinkle the rosemary sprigs over the potatoes. Toss gently to coat the potatoes and rosemary thoroughly with the oil. Spread the potatoes out in a single layer in the baking pan.

▣ Place the pan in the center of the oven and immediately reduce the heat to 375°F (190°C). Roast, stirring 2 or 3 times for even browning, until the potatoes are golden brown with crisp edges and tender when pierced with a fork, about 1 hour. Season to taste with salt and pepper.

▣ To serve, transfer to a warmed serving dish and serve immediately.

Serves 4

Baked Fennel

*Literally translated as cooking "in a bag," al cartoccio is a superb way to steam vegetables
in their own juices, with virtually no added fat. Here, fennel, a native of the Mediterranean,
comes out tender and moist, and with its licoricelike flavor wonderfully mellowed.*

2   fennel bulbs, about 2 lb (1 kg)
    total weight
1½ teaspoons extra-virgin olive oil
4   cloves garlic, lightly crushed
    (optional)
    Salt and ground white pepper

◈ Preheat an oven to 450°F (230°C).

◈ If the stalks and feathery tops of the fennel bulbs are still intact, cut them off and reserve for another use or discard. Trim the stem ends and remove any bruised outer leaves. Cut each bulb lengthwise into sixths; the core portion will hold each wedge intact. Coat one side of a large sheet of aluminum foil with the olive oil.

◈ Arrange the fennel wedges on the oiled side of the foil, tuck the garlic, if using, among the wedges and season to taste with salt and white pepper. Fold the foil over, bring the edges together and fold them over twice to make a double seal. Place on a baking sheet.

◈ Place the baking sheet on a rack in the center of the oven and immediately reduce the heat to 400°F (200°C). Bake for 15 minutes. Turn the pouch over and bake until fragrant and the fennel is tender when pierced with a fork, 10–15 minutes longer. To test for doneness, remove the pouch from the oven, unfold one corner and test with a fork. Seal and bake for a few more minutes longer if the fennel is not tender.

◈ To serve, remove the fennel from the pouch and transfer to a warmed serving dish. Serve warm.

Serves 4

Venetian-Style Beans with Swiss Chard

Combining beans, fresh herbs, anchovies and garlic, this Venetian side dish offers new flavors with every bite. Serve it as an antipasto *or a vegetarian* secondo piatto *accompanied with broiled mushrooms and tomatoes or steamed vegetables and garlic-rubbed bruschetta (recipe on page 20).*

BEANS

1½	cups (8 oz/250 g) dried borlotti or cranberry beans
1	carrot
1	celery stalk
½	yellow onion
1	bay leaf

DRESSING

4	tablespoons (2 fl oz/60 ml) extra-virgin olive oil
1	lb (500 g) Swiss chard leaves (silverbeet), stems trimmed and leaves cut into strips 2 inches (5 cm) wide
3	tablespoons minced shallots
2	tablespoons minced garlic
1	oil-packed anchovy fillet, rinsed and mashed (optional)
¾	cup (6 fl oz/180 ml) vegetable stock *(recipe on page 15)*
3	tablespoons chopped fresh parsley
2	tablespoons chopped fresh basil
2	teaspoons chopped fresh mint or 1 teaspoon dried mint
2	teaspoons chopped fresh sage or 1 teaspoon dried sage
2	teaspoons fresh thyme leaves or 1 teaspoon dried thyme
2	teaspoons fresh marjoram leaves or 1 teaspoon dried marjoram
1½	tablespoons red wine vinegar
	Salt and freshly ground pepper
	Chopped fresh basil or parsley

◆ To prepare the beans, sort through them and discard any misshapen beans or stones. Rinse and place in a bowl. Add water to cover and let stand for 2–3 hours. Drain. In a saucepan, combine the beans with water to cover. Bring to a boil, then drain immediately. Re-cover with water, again bring to a boil and drain.

◆ Return the beans to the pan and add the carrot, celery, onion, bay leaf and water just to cover. Bring to a boil, then reduce the heat to low and simmer, uncovered, until the beans are tender but not mushy, 25–30 minutes. Remove from the heat and let cool for 10 minutes, then drain and discard the liquid, vegetables and bay leaf. Set the beans aside.

◆ To make the dressing, in a frying pan over medium heat, warm 3 tablespoons of the olive oil. Add the Swiss chard and sauté until almost limp, 3–4 minutes. Add the remaining 1 tablespoon olive oil, the shallots and garlic and sauté until fragrant, about 30 seconds; do not allow to brown. Add the anchovy, if using, and stir for a few seconds until fragrant. Add the stock and bring to a boil. Add the reserved beans and stir until hot, 2–3 minutes.

◆ Add the parsley, basil, mint, sage, thyme and marjoram and stir until blended. Add the vinegar and stir for a few seconds to release the sharp vinegar fumes. Remove from the heat and season to taste with salt and pepper. Let cool, cover and refrigerate overnight to allow the flavors to develop.

◆ The next day, transfer to a serving dish, garnish with basil or parsley and serve at room temperature.

Serves 4

94

Sautéed Mushrooms with Onion, Garlic and Parsley

The term trifolati *comes from the old Umbrian word for truffle,* trifole, *suggesting the rich aromas that result from cooking any mushrooms with a mixture of onion, garlic, parsley and wine. Select a diverse mixture of fresh mushrooms, including white mushrooms, portobellos, cremini and any wild varieties. Serve as a side dish to roasted meats or spoon atop bruschetta (recipe on page 20) or veal scaloppine.*

1 package (¾ oz/20 g) dried porcini

1 cup (8 fl oz/250 ml) cool water

1 tablespoon extra-virgin olive oil

2 tablespoons minced yellow onion

1 tablespoon minced garlic

1 lb (500 g) assorted fresh mushrooms *(see note)*, stems removed, brushed clean and sliced

¼ cup (½ oz/15 g) minced fresh parsley

¼ cup (2 fl oz/60 ml) dry Italian white wine

Salt and freshly ground pepper

◼ In a bowl, combine the porcini and water. Let stand until softened, about 20 minutes. Remove the porcini, reserving the liquid. Clean the porcini, if needed, and chop coarsely. Strain the porcini liquid through a fine-mesh sieve lined with cheesecloth (muslin) into a clean container, then discard all but ¼ cup (2 fl oz/60 ml) of the liquid.

◼ In a frying pan over medium heat, warm the olive oil. When hot, add the onion and garlic and sauté until fragrant, about 30 seconds; do not allow to brown. Add the porcini and fresh mushrooms and continue to sauté over medium heat, stirring continuously to prevent burning, until slightly limp, about 3 minutes.

◼ Add the ¼ cup (2 fl oz/60 ml) reserved porcini liquid and simmer for 3 minutes. Add the parsley and white wine and simmer over medium heat until there is only ¼ cup (2 fl oz/60 ml) liquid remaining, 8–10 minutes.

◼ Season to taste with salt and pepper. Transfer to a warmed serving dish and serve immediately.

Serves 4

Sicilian Caponata with Pine Nuts and Raisins

This traditional Sicilian eggplant dish gets its delicate sweet-sour flavor from the combination of sugar, raisins, vinegar and capers. Every village on the island prepares its own version of the mixture, adding ingredients according to local custom.

1	large eggplant (aubergine), 1½ lb (750 g), unpeeled, cut into 1½-inch (4-cm) cubes
	Salt
	Sunflower or canola oil
1	yellow onion
1	zucchini (courgette)
2	celery stalks, cut into slices ½ inch (12 mm) thick
2	cups (16 fl oz/500 ml) quick tomato sauce *(recipe on page 15)*
3–4	teaspoons sugar
2	tablespoons red wine vinegar
¼	cup (1 oz/30 g) pine nuts
¼	cup (1½ oz/45 g) raisins
2	teaspoons capers, rinsed and patted dry (optional)
	Salt and freshly ground pepper

◙ Place the eggplant cubes in a colander and sprinkle with salt, tossing to coat evenly. Let stand for 1 hour to release any excess moisture. Pat dry with paper towels.

◙ In a large frying pan, pour in the oil to a depth of ½ inch (12 mm). Heat to 400°F (200°C) on a deep-fat frying thermometer, or until a cube of eggplant dropped into the oil begins to brown immediately. Add the eggplant and fry, turning, until golden on all sides, 12–15 minutes.

◙ Using a slotted spoon, transfer the eggplant to a colander to drain for about 20 minutes. Using paper towels, gently blot the eggplant to remove any excess oil. Set the eggplant aside. Pour off all but 1 tablespoon of the oil and set the frying pan aside; reserve the remaining oil for other uses.

◙ Cut the onion crosswise into 3 thick rings and then cut into 1-inch (2.5-cm) cubes. Quarter the zucchini lengthwise, then cut into 1-inch (2.5-cm) cubes.

◙ Place the frying pan used for cooking the eggplant over medium heat. Add the onion and sauté for 1 minute. Add the zucchini and sauté for another minute. Then stir in the celery and sauté for 1 minute longer. Stir in the tomato sauce and bring to a boil over medium heat, stirring occasionally. Add the eggplant, sugar to taste and vinegar and mix well. Reduce the heat to low and simmer, uncovered, until the sauce is thick and the vegetables are tender, 25–30 minutes.

◙ Meanwhile, toast the pine nuts. Preheat an oven to 325°F (165°C). Spread the nuts in a single layer on a baking sheet and toast, stirring occasionally, until golden, 8–10 minutes.

◙ Remove the eggplant mixture from the heat and stir in the toasted pine nuts, raisins and the capers, if using. Season to taste with salt and pepper. Let cool, then cover and chill for at least 1 day or for up to 3 days to blend the flavors.

◙ Before serving, using a large spoon, remove any oil that has solidified on the surface, then taste and adjust the seasonings. Serve at room temperature.

Serves 4

Desserts

A symbol of every family-operated trattoria are the pastries of *la nonna,* sweets made in the style of a grandmother and passed down through the generations. In many of Italy's best small restaurants, these pastries, along with other *dolci,* are presented on a long banquet table or a cart positioned in the center of the dining room to tempt visitors throughout the meal.

Seasonal fruits poached or made into a *sorbetto* or crisp *biscotti* dipped into dessert wines are favorite ways to conclude a meal. And although cheese is also increasingly popular as part of large repasts, it is more commonly offered as an *intermezzo*—that is, before the dessert.

A fresh peach *crostata,* filled with fruit marmalade and made with a traditional flaky butter pastry or a crispier olive oil–based alternative, exemplifies the Italian mastery of simple yet elegant desserts. Reserve the peach juice from the marmalade and use a few drops to flavor a sparkling white wine for enjoying along with the tart. A dessert of buttery lemon wafers, layered with a creamy filling that has been infused with chamomile and surrounded by berries, is an ideal conclusion to any summer meal, while a warm chocolate torte is the perfect ending for most winter repasts.

Sweet Gorgonzola with Baked Figs and Honey

Serving cheese as dessert, or just preceding dessert, is a European tradition. Here, the rich flavors of the cheese and the baked figs are offset by an extraordinary balance of sweet honey and the peppery nature of arugula. Select a sweet, not salty, cheese at its peak of ripeness. Offer thinly sliced walnut bread on the side and accompany with a sweet wine such as a Moscato or Malvasia.

4   firm yet ripe figs

1½   teaspoons extra-virgin olive oil

10   oz (315 g) sweet Gorgonzola cheese, rind removed and cut into 4 equal pieces

4   tablespoons (3 oz/90 g) acacia or wildflower honey

12   arugula (rocket) sprigs

▣ Preheat an oven to 475°F (245°C).

▣ Snip off the pointed tips of the figs and brush the fruits with the olive oil. Arrange in a small baking pan. Place in the center of the oven and immediately reduce the heat to 425°F (220°C). Bake until puffed and aromatic, about 10 minutes. Remove from the oven and let cool.

▣ Cut an X in the top of each fig and fold the corners back to resemble a flower, or split in half lengthwise. On each plate, attractively arrange 1 piece Gorgonzola, 1 fig and 3 arugula sprigs and drizzle with 1 tablespoon honey. Serve immediately.

Serves 4

Poached Autumn Pears with Mascarpone and Ginger

In Italy, autumn's choicest pears are often poached with sugar in a dry white or red wine. This recipe departs from convention, cooking them instead in a naturally sweet dessert wine. One of the best wines to use is Moscato d'Asti from Piedmont, which is made in both sparkling and still forms, and becomes a delicious honeylike syrup when reduced. If unavailable, any light, fruity dessert wine would do nicely.

POACHED PEARS

2	large ripe pears
1½	cups (12 fl oz/375 ml) Moscato d'Asti wine *(see note)*
1	stick cinnamon, 3 inches (7.5 cm) long, broken in half
½	teaspoon allspice berries or 1 whole clove

TOPPING

½	cup (3 oz/90 g) mascarpone cheese
2	teaspoons confectioners' (icing) sugar, or to taste
1	teaspoon milk
2	teaspoons chopped candied ginger
4	fresh mint sprigs, optional

To poach the pears, cut the pears in half lengthwise, then core and peel the halves. In a saucepan, combine the wine, cinnamon and allspice berries or the clove and bring to a boil.

Place the pears in the liquid, cored side down, reduce the heat to medium-low and simmer for 4–5 minutes. Turn the pears over and poach until barely soft when pierced with a sharp knife, 4–5 minutes longer. Using a slotted spoon, carefully place each pear half, cored side down, in the center of an individual plate.

Reduce the poaching liquid over medium heat until it forms a thick syrup, about 5 minutes. Strain through a fine-mesh sieve into a clean container. Discard the contents of the sieve.

To make the topping, in a small bowl, whisk together the mascarpone, sugar and milk until smooth.

To serve, cut each pear half into a fan shape: Hold a paring knife at a 45-degree angle to the pear, and make slashes completely through it, but leave the top intact. Gently press on the slices to spread them out, and then drizzle the reduced syrup over the top. Put a dollop of the mascarpone mixture at the top of each pear. Sprinkle evenly with the candied ginger and garnish with the mint sprigs, if desired.

Serves 4

Fresh Peach Tart

*Pasta frolla, the classic Italian pastry dough, may also be made with butter for a flakier crust: use
¾ cup (6 oz/185 g) chilled unsalted butter, cut into pieces, for the oil, only 1 egg and omit the vinegar.*

FILLING

3½ lb (1.75 kg) ripe yet firm
    yellow peaches, peeled, pitted
    and chopped

½   cup (4 oz/125 g) sugar or ⅓ cup
    (3½ oz/105 g) honey, or to taste

½   cup (4 fl oz/125 ml) dry Italian
    white wine

PASTRY

¼   cup (1 oz/30 g) slivered blanched
    almonds

½   cup (4 oz/125 g) sugar

2   cups (10 oz/315 g) all-purpose
    (plain) flour
    Pinch of baking soda (bicarbon-
    ate of soda)
    Pinch of salt

2   extra-large eggs

2   teaspoons vanilla extract (essence)

¾   teaspoon minced lemon zest

¾   teaspoon minced orange zest

⅓   cup (2½ fl oz/80 ml) mild-
    flavored extra-virgin olive oil

1   teaspoon distilled white vinegar

◫ To make the filling, in a bowl, toss together the peaches and sugar or honey; let stand for 1 hour. Then, in a saucepan, combine the peaches and wine. Bring to a boil, reduce the heat to low and simmer, uncovered, until soft, 60–70 minutes. Drain and let cool.

◫ To make the pastry, in a food processor fitted with the metal blade or in a blender, combine the almonds and a little bit of the sugar. Process until finely ground. If using a blender, pour the nut mixture into the bowl of an electric mixer. To the processor or mixer, add the remaining sugar, the flour, baking soda and salt. Pulse or beat briefly until blended.

◫ In a small bowl, whisk together the eggs, vanilla and lemon and orange zests; set aside. Turn the processor on or set the mixer on low speed (using a paddle attachment if you have one) and pour in the oil, then the vinegar, and finally the egg mixture, mixing for only a few seconds until a ball of dough forms. Divide into 2 portions, one twice as large as the other. Cover and refrigerate the smaller portion.

◫ Preheat an oven to 425°F (220°C). Place the larger dough portion between 2 sheets of flour-dusted waxed paper. Roll into a round about 11 inches (28 cm) in diameter and ⅛ inch (3 mm) thick. Peel off one piece of paper and transfer the round, paper side up, to a tart pan with a removable bottom 9 inches (23 cm) in diameter and 1¼ inches (3 cm) deep. Remove the remaining paper and press the pastry into the pan; trim off the overhang. Spread the filling over the pastry.

◫ Roll out the remaining dough portion in the same manner, forming a round 9 inches (23 cm) in diameter. Using a fluted or plain pastry wheel, cut into strips ½ inch (12 mm) wide. Using longer strips near the center, place half of the strips about ½ inch (12 mm) apart on top of the pie. Place the remaining strips at a right angle to the first strips, forming a lattice; trim off any overhang. Press the strips against the rim to seal securely.

◫ Place on a baking sheet and put in the center of the oven. Reduce the heat to 375°F (190°C) and bake for 25–30 minutes. Rotate the tart to ensure even browning and reduce the heat to 300°F (150°C). Continue to bake until the crust is golden and the filling puffs slightly, 20–25 minutes longer. Let cool before serving.

Makes one 9-inch (23-cm) tart; serves 8–10

Almond Biscotti

Biscotti means "twice-baked"; the first baking cooks the loaf of cookie dough and the second baking dries out and crisps the sliced cookies. Throughout Italy, an assortment of biscotti and other sweets are traditionally served with a glass of Vin Santo or an espresso or cappuccino for dipping.

½   cup (4 oz/125 g) unsalted butter, chilled

1   cup (8 oz/250 g) sugar

2   extra-large eggs, at room temperature

2⅓   cups (11½ oz/360 g) unbleached all–purpose (plain) flour

1   cup (4½ oz/140 g) slivered blanched almonds, chopped

2   teaspoons minced lemon zest

2   teaspoons fresh lemon juice

2¼   teaspoons aniseeds

1½   teaspoons baking powder

¼   teaspoon salt

1   tablespoon vanilla extract (essence)

1   teaspoon almond extract (essence)

◆ Preheat an oven to 375°F (190°C). Line 2 baking sheets with parchment (baking) paper.

◆ In a mixing bowl, using an electric mixer set on medium speed, beat together the butter and sugar until light and fluffy, 2–3 minutes. Beat in the eggs, one at a time, beating well after each addition. Gradually add the flour, beating until well mixed. Then add the almonds, lemon zest and juice, aniseeds, baking powder, salt, and vanilla and almond extracts and continue to beat until blended.

◆ Shape the dough into 4 logs, each one about 2 inches (5 cm) wide and ¾ inch (2 cm) high, and place on the prepared baking sheets. Place in the center of the oven and immediately reduce the heat to 325°F (165°C). Bake until light golden brown, puffy and a little firm when pressed on top, 25–30 minutes.

◆ Remove the baking sheets from the oven and immediately slice the logs crosswise on the sheets into pieces ½ inch (12 mm) thick. Separate the pieces on the sheets, keeping them upright and spacing them so that the air can circulate around them.

◆ Reduce the oven temperature to 275°F (135°C). Place the sheets in the center of the oven and bake until the biscotti are dry and crisp, 20–30 minutes. Transfer the biscotti to racks and let cool completely. Store in an airtight container.

Makes about 4 dozen cookies

Lemon Cialde with Chamomile Cream and Berries

Infused in cream, chamomile bestows its soothing character on an elegant dessert.
The recipe yields more wafers than you'll need for layering; store the remainder for teatime.

CHAMOMILE CREAM
1¼ cups (10 fl oz/310 ml) milk
1 tablespoon granulated sugar
4 extra-large egg yolks
3 chamomile tea bags
2 teaspoons powdered gelatin
2 tablespoons water
1 cup (8 fl oz/250 ml) heavy (double) cream, chilled

LEMON WAFERS
2 extra-large egg whites, at room temperature
½ cup (4 oz/125 g) granulated sugar
¼ cup (1½ oz/45 g) all-purpose (plain) flour
2 teaspoons minced lemon zest
¼ cup (2 oz/60 g) unsalted butter, melted and cooled

RASPBERRY SAUCE
1 cup (4 oz/125 g) raspberries
3–4 tablespoons confectioners' (icing) sugar, or to taste
1 tablespoon *grappa,* optional
1 cup (4 oz/125 g) strawberries, raspberries and/or blackberries, plus berries for garnish
3–4 teaspoons confectioners' (icing) sugar
Fresh mint leaves

To make the chamomile cream, in a small saucepan over medium heat, combine the milk and sugar and bring almost to a boil. Remove from the heat. In a small bowl, stir together the egg yolks until blended. Stir a few tablespoons of the hot milk into the yolks. Slowly pour the yolks into the hot milk, stirring continuously. Return to low heat and cook, stirring continuously, until thickened to a custard, 1–2 minutes; do not boil. Pour the custard through a fine-mesh sieve into a bowl. Add the tea bags and let stand for 30 minutes. Remove the tea bags, squeezing the liquid from them into the custard.

In a small pan over low heat, sprinkle the gelatin over the water; stir until dissolved. Pour into the custard and stir to mix. Let cool slightly.

Meanwhile, in a bowl, beat the cream until soft peaks form. Gently fold the cream into the cooled custard. Cover and refrigerate until firm, 4–6 hours or for up to 1 day.

To make the wafers, preheat an oven to 375°F (190°C). Butter and flour 2 baking sheets. In a clean bowl, beat the egg whites until soft peaks form. Slowly add the sugar and continue beating until the peaks are stiff and glossy, 3–4 minutes. Fold in the flour and lemon zest alternately with the melted butter just until blended. Let rest for 10 minutes.

For each wafer, using a spoon, place 2 teaspoons of the batter on a prepared baking sheet. Using the back of the spoon, spread into a disk 2¼ inches (5.5 cm) in diameter and ⅛ inch (3 mm) thick. You should have 24 disks in all. Place in the center of the oven and immediately reduce the heat to 325°F (165°C). Bake until pale gold and crisp, 10–12 minutes. While hot, using a spatula, carefully transfer to a rack to cool.

To make the sauce, in a food processor fitted with the metal blade, purée the raspberries. Pass through a fine-mesh sieve into a bowl. Stir in the sugar and the *grappa,* if using.

To assemble, set aside 12 of the wafers; store the remainder in an airtight container for another use. Spoon the custard into a pastry (piping) bag fitted with a star tip. Pipe a small dollop onto the center of a plate. Press a wafer on top. Pipe some custard over the center and arrange a row of berries around the edge. Cover with another wafer and again top with the custard and berries. Sprinkle a third wafer with ¾ teaspoon of the confectioners' sugar and place on top. Garnish with a swirl of custard, a berry and a mint leaf. Repeat until all have been assembled. Drizzle some berry sauce on each plate and serve immediately.

Serves 4

110

Tiramisù

*Literally translated "pick-me-up," tiramisù appropriately lightens the mood at the
end of any dinner party. Store-bought pound cake may be used instead of the ladyfingers,
and instant espresso or very strong coffee will do if an espresso machine is not at hand.*

5   extra-large egg yolks

5   tablespoons (2½ oz/75 g) sugar

1⅔ cups (13 oz/410 g) mascarpone
    cheese, chilled

1¾ cups (14 fl oz/440 ml) heavy
    (double) cream, chilled

¼   cup (2 fl oz/60 ml) brewed
    strong espresso, at room
    temperature

¼   cup (2 fl oz/60 ml) coffee-
    flavored liqueur

24 good-quality chocolate or plain
    ladyfingers
    Raspberries, optional
    Dutch-processed cocoa

◙ In a bowl, using an electric mixer set on high speed, beat together the egg yolks and sugar until pale yellow, smooth and shiny, 5–7 minutes. Add the mascarpone and beat until thickened and smooth, 3–4 minutes.

◙ In another bowl, using clean beaters or a whisk, whip the cream until soft peaks form. Using a rubber spatula or whisk, fold the whipped cream into the yolk mixture until thoroughly blended, breaking apart any lumps.

◙ In a small bowl, stir together the espresso and liqueur.

◙ Arrange the ladyfingers in a single layer over the bottom of a decorative serving bowl 10 inches (25 cm) in diameter. Brush some of the espresso mixture evenly over the ladyfingers. Turn the ladyfingers over and brush again until each one is almost soaked through with the espresso mixture. If using the raspberries, arrange around the edge. Spoon some of the mascarpone mixture over the ladyfingers to make an even layer ½ inch (12 mm) thick. Place the remaining ladyfingers in a single layer over the mascarpone and brush their tops with the remaining espresso mixture. Again, arrange raspberries around the edge, if using. Spoon the remaining whipped mascarpone on top, smoothing to cover completely. Cover and chill for at least 6 hours or for up to 2 days before serving.

◙ To serve, using a fine-mesh sieve, sift a light dusting of cocoa over the top. Using a large serving spoon, scoop portions of the tiramisù onto individual plates.

Serves 8

Plum Cake

Most trattorias take advantage of the abundance of seasonal fruits by offering them in desserts. In place of the plump summer plums that crown this delectable cake, you can use apricots, nectarines or blueberries. Whatever your selection, make sure the fruit is ripe but firm, as it will soften during baking.

6 tablespoons (3 oz/90 g) unsalted butter, at room temperature

⅓ cup (3 oz/90 g) plus 1 teaspoon granulated sugar

2 extra-large eggs, separated, at room temperature

1 cup (5 oz/155 g) unbleached all-purpose (plain) flour

2½ teaspoons baking powder

¼ cup (2 fl oz/60 ml) heavy (double) cream

¼ cup (2 fl oz/60 ml) water

2 teaspoons almond extract (essence)

1½ teaspoons vanilla extract (essence)

2 ripe plums, peeled, pitted and sliced into sixths
Confectioners' (icing) sugar

▣ Preheat an oven to 400°F (200°C). Butter and flour a 9-inch (23-cm) cake pan or a tart pan with a removable bottom.

▣ In a bowl, using an electric mixer set on medium speed, beat together the butter and the ⅓ cup (3 oz/90 g) granulated sugar until smooth and fluffy, 2–3 minutes. Add the egg yolks and beat until very smooth.

▣ In a small bowl, stir together the flour and baking powder. In another small bowl, stir together the cream, water and almond and vanilla extracts. Stir the flour mixture into the butter mixture alternately with the cream mixture, beginning and ending with the flour mixture. Do not overmix.

▣ In a clean bowl, using clean beaters, whip the egg whites until they form very soft peaks. Sprinkle in the 1 teaspoon granulated sugar and continue to beat until semisoft peaks form. Using a rubber spatula or whisk, fold the beaten egg whites into the batter, breaking apart any lumps. Pour the batter into the prepared pan and level the surface.

▣ Arrange the plums in a circle on the top of the batter. Place in the center of the oven and immediately reduce the heat to 350°F (180°C). Bake until the cake pulls away from the sides of the pan and a toothpick inserted into the center comes out clean, 35–40 minutes. Transfer to a rack and let cool slightly.

▣ If using a cake pan, run a knife blade around the edge of the pan to loosen the cake sides, invert onto the rack and then turn the cake right side up. If using a tart pan, remove the pan sides.

▣ Place the cake on a serving plate and using a fine-mesh sieve, sift confectioners' sugar evenly over the top. Serve warm or at room temperature.

Serves 8

Warm Chocolate Tortes with Raspberry Sauce

*Serve these miniature chocolate tortes soon after baking, as the warmth best
showcases their creamy, runny centers. For the smoothest texture and richest flavor,
purchase the best-quality European chocolate you can find.*

RASPBERRY SAUCE

1½	cups (6 oz/185 g) raspberries
3	tablespoons confectioners' (icing) sugar, or to taste

CHOCOLATE TORTES

3	teaspoons plus ¼ cup (2 oz/60 g) granulated sugar
3	oz (90 g) bittersweet (plain) chocolate
5	tablespoons (2½ oz/75 g) unsalted butter
3	extra-large egg yolks
1½	teaspoons minced orange zest
2	extra-large egg whites
¼	cup (1½ oz/45 g) all-purpose (plain) flour, sifted
¼	oz (7 g) white chocolate, cut into 8 pieces
1	small block white chocolate, for chocolate curls
	Raspberries

▨ To make the raspberry sauce, in a food processor fitted with the metal blade, purée the raspberries. Pass the purée through a fine-mesh sieve into a clean container. Stir in the confectioners' sugar.

▨ Preheat an oven to 425°F (220°C). To make the tortes, butter four standard-sized (½-cup/4-fl oz/125-ml) muffin tin cups, then sprinkle the bottom and sides with 2 teaspoons of the granulated sugar.

▨ Combine the bittersweet chocolate and butter in a heatproof bowl and set in a pan over (not touching) simmering water. Heat over medium heat, stirring continuously, just until the chocolate melts. Remove from the heat and let cool slightly.

▨ Meanwhile, in a bowl, using an electric mixer set on high speed, beat together the egg yolks and the ¼ cup (2 oz/60 g) granulated sugar until thick, about 4 minutes. Reduce the mixer speed to medium and slowly pour in the melted chocolate. Beat in the orange zest.

▨ In a clean bowl, using clean beaters, beat the egg whites until very soft peaks form. Sprinkle in the remaining 1 teaspoon granulated sugar and continue to beat until semisoft peaks form.

▨ Using a rubber spatula or whisk, fold the flour into the chocolate batter alternately with the egg whites, beginning and ending with the flour.

▨ Pour the batter into the prepared molds, filling to within ⅛ inch (3 mm) of the rims. Place 2 pieces of white chocolate on top of each mold; they will sink a little during baking.

▨ Place the pan in the center of the oven and immediately reduce the heat to 375°F (190°C). Bake until puffy and a thin but firm crust forms on top, 6–8 minutes. Do not open the oven door during the first 6 minutes of baking. Transfer the pan to a rack and let rest for 4–5 minutes to ease unmolding.

▨ Meanwhile, run a vegetable peeler along the block of white chocolate to form curls for garnishing the tortes. Keep the curls cool until serving.

▨ Run a sharp paring knife around the edge of each cup and quickly invert the tortes onto the rack. Transfer the tortes to individual plates, top sides down.

▨ Pour the raspberry sauce evenly over the tortes and then sprinkle with the chocolate curls. Scatter fresh raspberries around each torte. Serve immediately.

Serves 4

Chocolate-Hazelnut Torte

Candies, ice cream and tortes throughout Italy are flavored with gianduja, *the pleasing combination of hazelnuts and chocolate; those with the richest taste and most intense aroma come from Piedmont. This torte is typical of ones served in the charming Piedmontese town of Alba.*

1½ cups (7½ oz/225 g) hazelnuts (filberts)

1 cup (4 oz/125 g) confectioners' (icing) sugar

3 tablespoons potato starch (potato flour)

⅔ cup (3½ oz/105 g) unbleached all-purpose (plain) flour

1½ tablespoons unsweetened cocoa

2½ teaspoons baking powder
  Pinch of ground cinnamon

½ cup (4 oz/125 g) unsalted butter, cut into small pieces

2 extra-large eggs, lightly beaten, plus 1 extra-large egg yolk

2 teaspoons vanilla extract (essence)

◼ Preheat an oven to 325°F (165°C). Spread the hazelnuts in a single layer on a baking sheet and toast in the oven until they just begin to change color and the skins begin to loosen, 8–10 minutes. Spread the warm nuts on a kitchen towel. Cover with another kitchen towel and rub against the nuts to remove as much of the skins as possible. Let cool.

◼ Raise the oven temperature to 450°F (230°C). Butter and flour a cake pan 9 inches (23 cm) in diameter.

◼ In a food processor fitted with the metal blade or in a blender, combine ½ cup (2½ oz/75 g) of the peeled, cooled hazelnuts and the confectioners' sugar. Process just until the hazelnuts are finely ground, almost to a flour. (Do not overprocess.)

◼ In a bowl, combine the ground nut mixture, the potato starch, all-purpose flour, cocoa, baking powder and cinnamon. Using an electric mixer set on medium speed, beat for a few seconds to aerate the flour mixture. Add the butter and continue to beat until the butter is in very small pieces. Beat in the whole eggs and the egg yolk and the vanilla until blended.

Increase the speed to medium-high and beat until the mixture is fluffy and a light cocoa color, 2–3 minutes.

◼ Pour the batter into the prepared pan and level the surface. Place in the center of the oven and immediately reduce the heat to 400°F (200°C). Bake until a knife inserted in the center comes out clean, 30–35 minutes.

◼ While the cake is baking, place the remaining 1 cup (5 oz/150 g) hazelnuts in the food processor fitted with the metal blade or the blender. Process just until the hazelnuts are coarsely ground.

◼ When the cake is done, transfer it to a rack; let cool for 5 minutes. Run a sharp knife around the edge of the pan to loosen the cake sides and invert onto the rack. Then place, right side up, on a serving plate. Immediately sprinkle the ground hazelnuts evenly over the top and press lightly to adhere. Let cool completely and serve.

Serves 8

Cappuccino Gelato

The Saracens are credited with introducing ice cream to the Italians, who have made Italian gelato world famous. If you'd like this gelato to have a milder coffee flavor, make it with the mixture of espresso and liqueur known as caffè corretto. *The addition of both white and bittersweet chocolate, although optional, is irresistible.*

1½ cups (12 fl oz/375 ml) milk

½ cup (4 fl oz/125 ml) light (single) cream

¼ cup (2 oz/60 g) sugar

4 extra-large egg yolks

2 teaspoons vanilla extract (essence)

2 tablespoons instant espresso coffee powder dissolved in 1 tablespoon milk, or 3 tablespoons brewed espresso mixed with 1 tablespoon coffee-flavored liqueur

1 oz (30 g) white or bittersweet (plain) chocolate pieces, or a mixture, optional

Espresso-roast coffee beans or edible flowers, optional

▣ In a saucepan over medium heat, combine the milk, cream and sugar and stir to dissolve the sugar. Bring almost to a boil (190°F/88°C), then remove from the heat.

▣ In a small bowl, stir together the egg yolks until blended. Stir a few tablespoons of the hot milk into the yolks. Then slowly pour the yolks into the hot milk, stirring constantly. Place over low heat and cook, stirring, until thickened, 1–2 minutes. Do not allow to boil.

▣ Immediately pour the mixture through a fine-mesh sieve into a bowl to remove any lumps. Stir in the vanilla and one of the espresso mixtures. Let cool, cover and chill well, at least 2 hours.

▣ If desired, stir in the chocolate pieces, and then transfer to an ice cream maker. Freeze according to manufacturer's instructions.

▣ To serve, spoon into bowls and, if desired, top with coffee beans or garnish with fresh flowers.

Serves 4

Melon Sorbet

Italy's first melons came to ancient Rome from Persia. They were soon being cultivated successfully near the city, in the town of Cantalupo, which gave its name to today's best-known melon variety, showcased here in a light and refreshing sorbet. For the freshest flavor and best consistency, make the sorbet no more than 1 day in advance of serving.

¼ cup (2 fl oz/60 ml) water
¼ cup (2 oz/60 g) plus 1 teaspoon sugar
2½ lb (1.25 kg) cantaloupes
2 extra-large egg whites

◙ In a deep saucepan, combine the water and the ¼ cup (2 oz/60 g) sugar and bring to a boil over high heat. Do not stir or the mixture will crystallize. Continue to boil until it becomes a thick and clear syrup, about 5 minutes. Remove from the heat and let cool.

◙ Cut the cantaloupes in half, then remove and discard the seeds. Cut off and discard the rind. Chop the pulp coarsely. You should have about 1½ lb (750 g) pulp. Working in batches if necessary, place the melon pulp in a food processor fitted with the metal blade or in a blender and purée until smooth. Transfer the puréed melon to a bowl, add the cooled syrup and stir until blended. Cover and chill well, at least 2 hours.

◙ Transfer the melon mixture to an ice cream maker and freeze according to the manufacturer's instructions.

◙ Meanwhile, using a clean bowl and an electric mixer set at high speed, beat the egg whites until frothy. Add the 1 teaspoon sugar and continue to beat until semisoft peaks form.

◙ When the melon mixture is slushy and a little frozen, add the egg whites to the mixture and then continue to freeze until solid.

◙ To serve, spoon into bowls and serve immediately.

Serves 4

Glossary

The following glossary defines common ingredients and cooking terms, as well as special cooking equipment, used in trattorias.

Artichokes

These large flower buds of a variety of thistle, also known as globe artichokes, are native to the Mediterranean. When large, the tight cluster of tough, pointed leaves cover pale green inner leaves and a gray-green base—together comprising the heart, which conceals the prickly choke. In the springtime and early summer, Italians prize small, baby artichokes (below) just 1½–2 inches (4–5 cm) in diameter. These immature specimens require only light trimming of their bases and tougher outer leaves before they are steamed whole or sliced to serve raw in salads.

TO TRIM ARTICHOKES

Cut off the stem and top half of each large artichoke. Remove the tough outer leaves and, using a small sharp knife, trim away the fibrous green layer at the base of the artichoke. Cut large artichokes lengthwise into quarters and cut away the prickly choke; leave small artichokes whole.

TO STEAM ARTICHOKES

Place the trimmed artichokes on a steamer rack over (not touching) boiling water. Cover and steam until tender when pierced with a fork, 5–7 minutes. Remove the artichokes from the rack and let cool.

Arugula

Also known as rocket, this green leaf vegetable has slender, multiple-lobed leaves and a peppery, slightly bitter flavor. Used raw in salads and cooked in pasta sauces.

Beans

Beans are popular rustic fare throughout Italy. Before use, dried beans should be carefully picked over to remove small stones or fibers or any discolored or misshapen beans. Soaking them in cold water for several hours rehydrates them and thus shortens their cooking time.

Some popular varieties used in this book are:

Borlotti Medium-sized dried beans, shaped like kidney beans, with speckled pink or beige skins. Substitute pink kidney beans or pinto beans.

Cannellini Small, white, thin-skinned oval beans. Great Northern or white (navy) beans may be substituted.

Cranberry Small, full-flavored, mealy-textured beans with mottled cranberry-and-tan skins. Pinto beans may be substituted.

Belgian Endive

This white to pale yellow-green leaf vegetable is characterized by its refreshing, slightly bitter, spear-shaped leaves, which are tightly packed in cylindrical heads 4-6 inches (10-15 cm) long. Used raw or cooked. Also known as chicory or witloof.

Breads

To serve with authentic trattoria-style meals, or for bread crumbs, choose a good rustic loaf made from unbleached wheat flour, with a firm, coarse crumb.

TO MAKE BREAD CRUMBS

When a recipe calls for fresh bread crumbs, cut off the crusts from a good-quality loaf with a firm, coarse crumb. Crumble the bread into a food processor fitted with the metal blade. Process until small crumbs form. Store in an airtight container in the freezer to use as needed.

Capers

Capers, the buds of a common Mediterranean bush, grow wild all over Italy. For use as a savory flavoring ingredient, they are first preserved in salt, or more commonly, pickled in salt and vinegar.

Cheeses

Scores of different cheeses are produced in Italy. Among the most popular varieties, used in this book, are:

Caciotta A creamy, semihard cheese ranging from mild to slightly tangy when aged. Made from all sheep's milk or a blend of sheep and cow's milk. Some varieties include dolce sardo from Sardinia, caciotta toscana from Tuscany and pientino from Pienza.

Emmenthaler This common variety of Swiss cheese has a firm, smooth texture, large holes, and a mellow, slightly sweet and nutty flavor.

Gorgonzola A specialty of Lombardy, Gorgonzola is named for a town just outside of Milan. This mild, creamy, pale yellow blue-veined cheese is made from fresh cow's milk. Some Gorgonzola tends to be salty. Milder varieties are labeled dolcelatte, literally "sweet milk." Other blue cheeses may be substituted.

Mascarpone A thick, fresh cream cheese traditionally sold in small tubs. Similar to French crème fraîche, it is used to enrich sauces or desserts; it may also be sweetened and flavored to be eaten alone.

Mozzarella Mild, rindless white cheese, traditionally made from water buffalo's milk and sold fresh. Commercially produced and packaged cow's milk mozzarella is now much more common, although it has less flavor. Look for fresh mozzarella sold immersed in water. Small, bite-sized balls of the cheese are known as bocconcini. It may also be flavored and preserved by smoking, giving it a firmer texture and a deep yellowish-brown color.

Parmesan With a sharp, salty, full flavor acquired during at least two years of aging, the best examples of this hard, thick-crusted cow's milk cheese are prized among cooks and diners alike. Although it takes its name from the city of Parma, Parmesan originated midway between that city and Reggio, where the finest variety, Parmigiano Reggiano®, is produced. Buy in block form, to grate fresh as needed.

Pecorino Italian sheep's milk cheese, sold either fresh or aged. Among its most popular aged forms is pecorino romano from Rome and its vicinity.

Provolone Fairly firm cheese made either from cow's or water buffalo's milk. It is pale yellow and its flavor ranges from mild and slightly sweet to strong and tangy.

Ricotta A light, mild and soft fresh cheese made from twice-cooked milk—traditionally sheep's milk, although cow's milk ricotta is far more common today. Sold in small tubs in most markets.

Chilies

Centuries ago, Italians adopted the New World's varied chili peppers as a source of mild-to-hot spiciness. Small red chilies are sold fresh or dried.

Eggplant

Tender, mildly earthy, sweet vegetable-fruit covered with tough, shiny skin, which may be peeled or left on in long-cooked dishes. Eggplants vary in color from the familiar purple to red and from yellow to white. The most common variety is the large, purple globe eggplant (below), but many markets also carry the slender, purple Asian variety, which is more tender and has fewer, smaller seeds. Also known as aubergine.

Fennel

This crisp, refreshing, anise-flavored bulb vegetable is sometimes sold under its Italian name, *finocchio*. The bulb, with its fine, feathery leaves and stems, is sold separately from the small yellowish-brown fennel seeds.

Garlic

This intensely aromatic bulb has helped to define the character of Italian cooking since ancient times. To ensure the best flavor, buy whole heads of dry garlic, separating individual cloves from the head as needed, and do not purchase more than you will use in 1 or 2 weeks.

TO PEEL A GARLIC CLOVE
Place it on a work surface and cover it with the side of a large knife. Press down firmly but carefully on the side of the knife to crush it slightly; the skin will slip off easily.

Hazelnuts

Also known as filberts, these small, spherical nuts have a special affinity with chocolate, and are teamed with it in many Italian sweets.

Herbs

A wide variety of fresh and dried herbs add complex aromatic character to foods. Some popular herbs include:

Basil A sweet, spicy herb used both dried and fresh.

Bay Leaf The dried leaves of the bay laurel tree give their pungent, spicy flavor to sauces and other simmered dishes.

Marjoram Pungent and aromatic, this herb may be used dried or fresh to season lamb and other meats, poultry, seafood, vegetables or eggs.

Oregano Oregano is noted for its aromatic, spicy flavor, which intensifies with drying. Also known as wild marjoram.

Parsley Although this popular fresh herb is available in two varieties, Italian cooks prefer flat-leaf parsley, also known as Italian parsley, which has a more pronounced flavor than the more common curly-leaf type.

Rosemary Used either fresh or dried, strong-flavored rosemary frequently scents meat dishes, as well as seafood and vegetables. Use it sparingly, except when grilling.

Sage Fresh or dried, this pungent herb goes well with pork, lamb, veal or poultry.

Thyme Delicately fragrant and clean tasting, this small-leaved herb is used fresh or dried to flavor savory dishes.

Juniper Berries

The aromatic dried berries of the juniper tree. Commonly used in pickling mixtures and to season poultry and game.

Leeks

These sweet, moderately flavored members of the onion family are long and cylindrical, with a pale white root end and dark green leaves.

Mortadella

A specialty of Bologna, this wide, air-cured, mottled pork sausage has a mildly spicy flavor and fine texture.

Mushrooms

With their rich, earthy flavors and meaty textures, mushrooms inspire passion in Italian cooks and diners alike. Most are available either fresh or dried; rehydrate dried mushrooms before using. Some types used in this book include:

Cremini Similar in size and shape to common cultivated white mushrooms, this variety has a more pronounced flavor and a rich brown skin concealing creamy tan flesh.

Porcini These rich, meaty wild mushrooms are also known by the French term *cèpe*.

Portobello Fully mature cremini mushrooms, portobellos (below, left) are noted for their wide, flat, deep brown caps and rich, mildly meaty taste.

Shiitake Meaty in flavor and texture, these Asian mushrooms (below, right) have flat, dark brown caps 2–3 inches (5–7.5 cm) wide.

White These common cultivated mushrooms come in three sizes, from the smallest, or button (below, center), to cup, to the largest, or flat mushrooms.

Nutmeg

The hard pit of the fruit of the nutmeg tree, this spice may be bought already ground or, for fresher flavor, whole, to be ground on a nutmeg grater (below), as needed.

Olive Oil

Olive oil predominates in the cooking of Italy's warmer regions, from the Ligurian coast and Tuscany southward.

Extra-virgin olive oil, extracted from olives on the first pressing without use of heat or chemicals, is valued for its distinctive fruity flavor. Products labeled pure olive oil are less aromatic and flavorful and may be used for general cooking purposes.

Olives

In Italy, particularly in the more southerly regions with harsher soil, olive trees thrive. Ripe black and underripe green olives are cured in combinations of salt, seasonings, brines, oils and vinegars to produce a wide range of piquant and pungent results. If Italian varieties called for in the recipes in this book are unavailable, substitute similar Italian or Greek cured olives.

Pancetta

This unsmoked bacon is cured simply with salt and pepper. Available in Italian delicatessens and specialty-food stores, it may be sold flat, although it is commonly available sliced from a large sausage-shaped roll.

Pasta Machine

The classic Italian device for making pasta at home is a hand-cranked stainless-steel machine that passes fresh pasta dough between a pair of adjustable rollers (**A**).

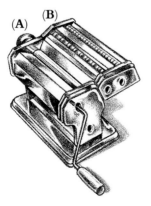

Set at their widest distance, the rollers are used to knead the dough; then the distance between them is progressively narrowed as the dough is passed through at each setting until the desired thinness is reached. For flat cuts, the sheet of dough is then cranked through a cutting attachment (**B**) to produce strands.

Pine Nuts

Often referred to by their Italian name, *pinoli,* these small, ivory nuts are the seeds of a species of pine tree, and have a rich, resinous flavor.

Polenta

Imperial Roman soldiers ate *pulmentum,* a mush of millet, chick-pea (garbanzo) flour or spelt. Down through the ages, this gruel—its name evolved to the Italian polenta—incorporated other grains, eventually settling on corn, which began to gain popularity in Italy in the late 17th century. Today, the term refers not only to the mush but also to the cornmeal from which it is made.

Prosciutto

A specialty of Parma, this raw ham is cured by dry-salting for 1 month, then air-drying in cool curing sheds for 6 months or longer. Used as an ingredient, it is also served as an antipasto, cut into tissue-thin slices that highlight its deep pink color.

Radicchio

The most common variety has small reddish purple leaves with creamy white ribs, formed into an elongated sphere. Radicchio may be served raw in salads, or cooked, usually by grilling. Also called red chicory.

Rice

Rice has been a significant crop in Italy since the 16th century. By general consensus, the best Italian rice is grown in the Piedmont and Lombardy, with short, round grains such as Arborio, Vialone Nano and Carnaroli prized for the creamy consistency and chewy texture they give to risotto. Italians also cook with long-grain white rice, the slender grains of which steam to a light, fluffy consistency.

Saffron

This intensely aromatic, golden orange spice was introduced to Italy by the Spanish in the 16th century. Made from the dried stigmas of a species of crocus, saffron perfumes and imparts a golden hue to many dishes. Whether you buy it as threads—the dried stigmas—or in powdered form, purchase only those products labeled pure saffron.

Scallops

Bivalve mollusks with rich, slightly sweet flesh. Sea scallops are shaped like plump discs about 1½ inches (4 cm) in diameter, while bay scallops are considerably smaller. Usually sold already shelled. Remove the tough muscle, or foot, from sea scallops before using.

Shallots

These small cousins of the onion have a papery brown skin, purple-tinged flesh and a flavor resembling both sweet onion and garlic.

Shrimp

Before cooking, fresh shrimp (prawns) are usually peeled and their thin, veinlike intestinal tracts removed.

TO PEEL AND DEVEIN FRESH SHRIMP

Use your thumbs to split open the thin shell along the concave side, between the legs, then carefully peel it away (below). Using a small, sharp knife, make a shallow slit along the shrimp's back to expose the veinlike, usually dark intestinal tract. Using the tip of the knife or your fingers, lift up and pull out the vein.

Tomatoes

Introduced from the New World to Italy in the mid-16th century, tomatoes were not popular in Italian kitchens until the 18th century. Today, they find their way into every course of the meal except dessert.

The most familiar variety, and those that offer the best quality year-round, are Italian plum tomatoes (above, right), also known as Roma or egg tomatoes. Canned whole plum tomatoes are the most reliable for cooking; those designated San Marzano are considered the finest. At the peak of summer, firm, sun-ripened beefsteak tomatoes (below, left) are an excellent choice for using fresh. Ripe tomatoes are also dried in the sun and submerged in olive oil or packaged dry; the latter may be reconstituted by soaking them in cool water.

TO PEEL FRESH TOMATOES

Bring a saucepan of water to a boil. Using a small, sharp knife, cut out the core from the stem end and cut a shallow X at the tomato's base. Submerge the tomato for about 20 seconds in the boiling water, then remove and cool in a bowl of cold water. Working from the X, peel off the skin, using your fingertips or the knife blade.

TO SEED TOMATOES

Cut them in half crosswise and squeeze to force out the seeds.

Vinegars

The term *vinegar* refers to any alcoholic liquid caused to ferment a second time by certain strains of yeast, turning it highly acidic. Vinegars highlight the qualities of the liquid from which they are made. Red wine vinegar, for example, has a more robust flavor than vinegar produced from white wine. Balsamic vinegar, a specialty of Modena since well before the 11th century, is made from reduced grape juice and is aged and blended for many years in a succession of casks made of different woods and gradually diminishing in size. The result is a tart-sweet, intensely aromatic vinegar.

Zest

The thin outer layer of a citrus fruit's peel contains most of its aromatic oils, which can provide lively flavor to both sweet and savory dishes. You can remove the zest with a simple tool known as a zester, drawn across the fruit's skin to cut the zest in thin strips; with a fine hand-held grater; or in wide strips with a vegetable peeler or a paring knife held almost parallel to the fruit's skin. For finely minced zest, use a small, sharp knife to mince the strips.

Zucchini

A squash of the New World, the slender, cylindrical green zucchini long ago found its way into Italian kitchens. Seek out smaller zucchini, which have a finer texture and tinier seeds than more mature specimens. Italian cooks who grow them in their own gardens take care to save the delicate blossoms, stuffing them for an *antipasto;* in the spring, well-stocked produce markets often sell zucchini with their blossoms still attached.

Acknowledgments

Mary Beth Clark would like to extend her thanks to Carol Amon, Rita A. Clark, Eugene V. Clark and William E. Ente.

For lending photographic props, the photographer and stylist would like to thank:

David Jones, Sydney, NSW

Art of Food and Wine, Woollahra, NSW

Accoutrement, Mosman, NSW

Appley Hoare Antiques, Woollahra, NSW

Bay Tree, Woollahra, NSW

Alison Coates Flowers, Paddington, NSW

Georg Jensen, Sydney, NSW

Royal Copenhagen, Artarmon, NSW

Marble Factory, Matraville, NSW

For their valuable editorial support, the publishers would like to thank: Ken DellaPenta, Liz Marken, Stephani Grant, Marguerite Ozburn, Claire Sanchez, Maria Triaca and Laurie Wertz.

Photo Credits

Pages 2-3:
Roberto Soncin Gerometta/ Photo 20-20

Page 7:
Peter Johnson

Page 8:
Andrea Pistolesi/ Image Bank (bottom left)
Fred Lyon (top right)

Page 9:
Michael Freeman (bottom left)
Fred Lyon (right)

Index

TRATTORIA: THE BEST OF CASUAL ITALIAN COOKING